This book belongs to

....

First published in 2010 by Miles Kelly Publishing Ltd
Harding's Barn, Bardfield End Green, Thaxted, Essex, CM6 3PX, UK

This edition printed 2015

8 10 12 14 15 13 11 9

Publishing Director *Belinda Gallagher*
Creative Director *Jo Cowan*
Editor *Carly Blake*
Designer *Michelle Cannatella*
Cover Designer *Rob Hale*
Consultant *Janet Dyson*
Production *Elizabeth Collins, Caroline Kelly*
Reprographics *Stephan Davis, Jennifer Cozens*
Assets *Lorraine King*

ISBN 978-1-78209-518-7

Printed in China

British Library Cataloguing-in-Publication Data
A catalogue record for this book is available from the British Library

ACKNOWLEDGEMENTS
The publishers would like to thank the following artists
who have contributed to this book:

The Bright Agency: Katriona Chapman, Dan Crisp,
Giuliano Ferri, Mélanie Florian (inc. cover)

Advocate Art: Andy Catling, Alida Massari

The publishers would like to thank:
Robert Willoughby and the London School of Theology for their help in compiling this book.
The pupils of Northbury Junior School, Essex, for their valuable contribution.

Every effort has been made to acknowledge the source and
copyright holder of each picture. Miles Kelly Publishing
apologises for any unintentional errors or omissions.

Made with paper from a sustainable forest

www.mileskelly.net
info@mileskelly.net

100 Bible Stories

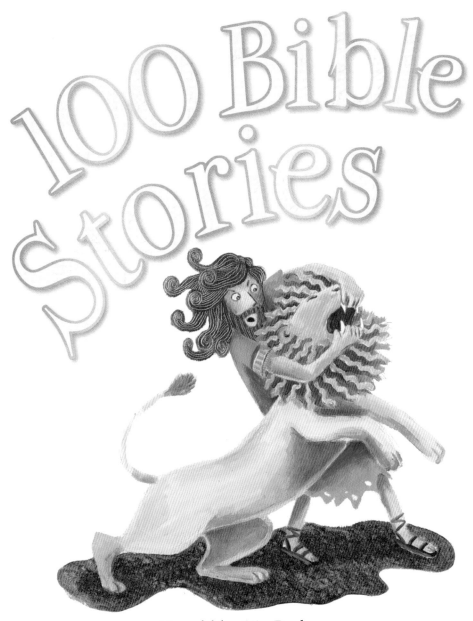

Retold by Vic Parker

Miles
KeLLY

INTRODUCTION

The Bible is often described as the world's
best-selling book, however it is more like an entire
library. It is made up of sixty-six individual books,
and split into two sections known as the Old
Testament and the New Testament. The Bible is
believed by countless readers all over the world to
be the Word of God. It was written by many people
over more than one thousand years, from about
1450 BC. Originally written in Hebrew, Aramaic
and Greek, the Bible has been translated
into many different languages.

The books contain detailed historical information, ancient proverbs and laws, songs, poetry, personal letters and diaries, stirring adventures of heroes and heroines and marvellous tales of miracles and mystery. These writings teach us all about God, while entertaining and delighting us at the same time. Many captivating Bible characters and their colourful stories have become lifelong favourites of millions of children. We hope that the wonderful tales retold here will become yours, too.

Story Categories

The stories are divided into six different categories, or groups. Each group has its own icon, or symbol, which can be seen at the top of the pages. For example, if you want to read stories from the Mysteries and Marvels category, look for the pages with the yellow sun icon.

 Mysteries and Marvels

 Families and Friends

 Sin and Salvation

 Walking God's Path

 Voices and Visions

 Heroes and Villains

Contents

The Old Testament

THE NEW TESTAMENT

The Old Testament

The Old Testament is the name for the first section of the Bible, made up of thirty-nine books written over two thousand years ago. They were compiled by Jewish people who lived in the Middle East (where parts of Israel, Palestine, Lebanon, Syria, Jordan and Egypt are today). The books describe the Jews' special relationship with God over hundreds of years, beginning with the creation of the world. The Jews made many careful copies of the original ancient manuscripts, so the writings of the Old Testament were never lost. They contain family trees, religious laws, poetry, hymns and stories that narrate the events of hundreds of characters.

The Creation of the World

In the beginning, God lived in darkness. There was nothing else except for a vast ocean that rushed and raged over a mass of land that lay beneath. Then God had an idea. "Let there be light!" He said, and mysteriously there was. God liked the brightness. He enjoyed it for a while and then called the darkness back for another turn. That was the very first day and night.

When God lit up the second day, He had another idea. "I want a roof to arch over everything, way up high!" He said, and all at once there was one. Then He parted the ocean, scooped up half of the water and poured it out onto the roof. The swirling patterns that formed above were beautiful. God gave the roof a special name – sky.

God looked down at the remaining water boiling and bubbling below. "Move aside so the land can show through!" He ordered, and it did. The land rose up and the water swirled around it. God was very pleased and decided to call them earth and sea. But He thought the land looked too bare. God imagined grass and flowers and bushes and trees. Before the third day ended, they were growing all over the earth.

On day number four, God decorated the sky. In it He hung a blazing, hot light called the sun, a pale, cold light called the moon and millions of burning, twinkling stars. Then He set them all moving around each other in a way that would mark out the passing of the days, nights, seasons and years.

Next, God looked over His creation and decided that He wanted things to live in it. He spent the fifth day imagining all sorts of creatures that floated, swam and dived in the water, and that soared, hovered and buzzed in the air. Suddenly, the sea was

17

filled with fish and sea creatures and the air was busy with birds and insects.

On the sixth day, God imagined creatures that galloped, hopped and slithered. Creatures with fur, scales and shells, and with claws, hooves and horns. Creatures that barked, hissed, howled and grunted. All at once, the earth was alive with all kinds of animals.

Last of all, God took a handful of earth and modelled it into a figure that looked just like Him. He bent down and breathed into the figure's nostrils. It shivered, blinked and came alive, and looked at Him. It was the first man, Adam. God quickly realized that the man would be lonely all on his own, so He sent him into a deep sleep while

He made him a companion. God gently took out one of the man's ribs and healed up the wound. Then He shaped the rib into another, similar figure – the first woman, Eve. Finally, God brought Eve to life, then woke up Adam and introduced them to each other. God watched His two humans with delight as they spoke and got to know each other. God was so thrilled with them that He put them in charge of all the other living things He had made. He even planted a beautiful garden especially for Adam and Eve to live in, in a place called Eden.

At last, God sat back and looked at the world He had created. He had used every colour, shape and texture, and every size, sound and scent that He could think of.

God was very pleased with everything, and decided that He had done enough. He spent the seventh day relaxing after all His efforts. God ordered that from then on, every seventh day should be a special day of rest in memory of when He had completed His wonderful work.

And that is how the world was made.

Genesis chapters 1, 2

Adam and Eve in the Garden of Eden

God made sure that the Garden of Eden had everything that Adam and Eve needed to be happy. The sun kept them warm, so they didn't need clothes – they weren't embarrassed about being naked anyway. A gushing stream gave them water. All sorts of flowers, plants and trees grew

there, fragrant and shady, and
bearing tasty fruits, nuts and seeds.
   In the middle of the garden grew the
two most beautiful trees of all – the Tree
of Life and the Tree of Knowledge.

   "Take care of my marvellous garden,"
God told Adam and Eve. "Enjoy eating
anything you like, except for the fruits of
the Tree of Knowledge. Please do not eat
those. If you do, you will die."

   Adam and Eve did as they were told and
their life in the garden was wonderful, until
one day Eve met a snake. The snake was by
far the most cunning of all the creatures
God had made. Very slyly, it asked Eve,
"Did God really tell you not to eat from
one of the trees?"

"Yes, that one," replied Eve, pointing to the Tree of Knowledge. "He said that if we do, we'll die. I don't think we're even allowed to touch it."

"Nonsense," hissed the snake. "You won't die! God doesn't want you to eat that fruit because if you do, you'll become like Him. You'll know the difference between good and bad, just as He does."

Eve gazed nervously at the Tree of Knowledge. How beautiful it was! Its leaves whispered mysteriously in the breeze and its branches stretched towards her. Its fruits hung down, ripe and ready to drop into her hand. "How wonderful it would be to become wise!" Eve murmured. Overcome with longing, she reached out, picked the nearest fruit and took a big, juicy bite. It was so delicious! Surely something that tasted so good could not be wrong. Eve hurried to share the fruit with Adam and he couldn't resist trying it either.

Suddenly, Adam and Eve realized that they did indeed know the difference between good and bad – and what they had done was very wrong. The couple felt dreadfully ashamed and were embarrassed about being naked too. They tried to sew leaves together to cover themselves. Then, in horror, they heard God coming. Quickly, they hid, but God knew.

"Adam," God called, "why are you and Eve hiding from me?"

The red-faced couple crept out, hanging their heads.

"We were frightened when we heard You, and also we weren't dressed," Adam mumbled.

"What has made you want clothes? And why are you afraid of me?" God demanded. "You haven't eaten the fruit I asked you not to eat, have you?"

Adam owned up, but he blamed it all on Eve, who in turn blamed the snake. God listened as they squirmed and squabbled. Then with huge disappointment He said, "I have no choice but to punish you all."

He sent the snake crawling away in the dust, the enemy of humans forever. After making animal-skin clothes for Adam and Eve, He turned them out of their beautiful garden home. "From now on, you will have to fend for yourselves and struggle to grow food," God told them. "And one day, you will go back to being the earth from which I made you – you will one day die." He set angels with fiery swords to guard the Tree of Life, so that Adam and Eve could not eat its fruit to save themselves from eventually dying. God watched in great sadness as the shamed couple walked out into the world.

Genesis chapters 2, 3

The World's First Crime

After Adam and Eve had been cast out from the Garden of Eden, their life was hard and harsh. However God made sure it wasn't always all struggle and sorrow. In time He sent the couple children and they were overjoyed. The first baby born to Eve was a little boy whom they called Cain.

Their second was also a boy, whom they named Abel. Both sons grew up to be healthy, strong and hard-working. Cain became a farmer, while Abel chose to be a shepherd. However the two young boys had very different personalities. Abel was good-natured, kind and caring, but his big brother Cain was bad-tempered and moody.

Things came to a head one day when Cain and Abel paid their respects to God. They each prayed and offered Him a gift. Abel selected the finest and fattest of his sheep for his offering to God, and Cain delivered the very best of his crops and fruit. God was highly pleased with Abel, but He not only turned down Cain's offering, He also told him off.

Instead of being ashamed, Cain was furious and his face looked like thunder.

"Why are you so angry? And why have you got that scowl on your face?" God demanded. "If you behave well, of course I'll be happy to accept your offerings."

Cain stomped off, totally fed up with God and burning with jealousy of his younger brother. He could have thought about what God had said and tried to turn over a new leaf – but he didn't. Instead, He allowed himself to be swallowed up by anger and hatred and all he could think of was hurting his brother.

Cain plotted how to do this. He invited Abel to go with him to some distant fields deep in the countryside, where they were all alone. There, Cain suddenly turned on his younger brother in a vicious attack and soon Abel was lying dead on the ground.

Cain coolly returned home as though nothing had happened. He was sure that no one had seen him and that he would get away with his terrible crime, but of course God knew everything that he had done.

"Cain, where is your brother?" God challenged.

"How do I know?" Cain replied rudely. "I am not my brother's keeper."

Then God boomed, "Cain, what have you done? I can see your brother's blood staining the earth red. It is crying out to me, telling of your dreadful deed! From now on, the earth will not grow anything for you ever again. I am sending you to live far away, where I no longer have to look at you. You can wander homeless for the rest of your days!"

Cain fell to his knees in despair. "Please, God," he sobbed. "That's a terrible punishment. Not only are you driving me from my home and all that I know, you are sending me to certain death. If strangers find me, wandering hungry and helpless, they're bound to kill me."

But God had had enough of violence and murder. He put a special mark on Cain that commanded that no one hurt him. Then God sent him away, far beyond Eden, to a distant eastern land called Nod.

Poor Adam and Eve had lost their first two children, but God took pity on them once more. He sent Eve other babies, beginning with a third son, Seth. And so the couple were comforted, and lived to such a great old age that they had the happiness of seeing many generations of grandchildren born to them.

Genesis chapter 4

Noah and the Ark

As the years went by, Adam and Eve's many great-great-grandchildren had many great-great-grandchildren of their own. People spread all over the world. They quite forgot that they were part of one big family. They also forgot about God and began behaving badly in all sorts of ways.

God looked down from Heaven and became more and more sad and angry. Eventually, people became so selfish and cruel that God was sorry He had ever created the human race. He decided the best thing was to remove everybody and start all over again.

Well, not quite everybody. There was just one person in the world who tried to live a good, honest, hard-working life – a farmer called Noah. God decided to save Noah, his wife and three sons, Shem, Ham and Japheth, and their wives.

God spoke to Noah and told him about His terrible decision. "Look around you, Noah. Everyone in the world is evil, and I have had enough. I am going to wash everybody off the face of the earth, but I promise, you and your family will be safe. Here's what you have to do. I want you to build a huge, covered boat – an ark. Use the best wood you can find and build it 133 metres long, 22 metres wide and 13 metres high, with a roof of reeds. Coat the whole thing with tar, inside and out, so that it is watertight. Give it a door and windows and build three decks divided into compartments. When I tell you, load up the ark with one pair of every living creature – a male and a female. Take seven pairs of animals you can eat because you'll need enough food to feed you all. I am going to send forty days and forty nights of rain to flood the whole world."

Noah told his family and they hurried to begin the enormous task. Their neighbours thought they were mad as they began building the huge ship. How people laughed! But Noah and his family trusted God and kept working, and after many months the ark was finished. The day came when God warned Noah to begin loading the animals into the ark and settling his family onboard. A week later, thunder clouds blackened the skies, blotting out the sun, and it began to rain.

Genesis chapters 6, 7

The Great Flood

The rain that God sent to flood the world was like nothing anyone had seen before or could have imagined. It was as if the sky had shattered and through the cracks plunged mighty waterfalls. As the rain poured down, rivers burst their banks, lakes flooded their valleys, oceans swelled and overflowed and the ark floated off on the rising waters. Towering tidal waves rushed over the land, drowning everything in their path and still the rain continued. The ark was lashed and battered, and hurled this way and that by the currents.

The rain fell for forty days and nights just as God had said. Then as quickly as it had started, it stopped. When Noah dared to peep out, he could see nothing but water in all directions.

Over the quiet, empty days that followed, the sun began to dry up the water and the flood gradually started to sink. God sent a great wind to speed things along. Eventually, the ark groaned and shuddered as it scraped along the ground and came to a halt on top of Mount Ararat in Turkey.

Noah didn't dare leave the ark yet. He waited a few days for the waters to sink further, then sent a raven into the sky. The raven soared back and forth and all it could see was water. Noah waited a week, then sent out a dove. It flew back the same day and Noah knew that there was not enough land showing yet. He waited another week, then sent the dove out again. That evening it returned, carrying an olive leaf. The waters were low enough to show land where trees grew! Noah waited one week more and again sent out the dove. This time it did not return. Nervously, Noah opened the door and the ark was surrounded by dry land!

Then God called, "Noah, it's time for you and your family to go out into the world with the creatures and begin again." And that's what they did. God was pleased and blessed Noah and his family. He vowed that He would never again send a flood to destroy the living things He had created. God set a rainbow in the sky as a sign to always remind everyone of His promise.

Genesis chapters 7 to 9

The Tower
of Babel

In the early days of the world people lived much longer than they do now. The Bible says that Noah was six hundred years old at the time of the flood and that he didn't die until he was nine hundred and fifty! Noah lived to see his sons and their wives have many children, grandchildren and

generations of great-grandchildren. The
family grew so big that there were many
thousands of people in the world again, just
as God had wished.

Of course, people travelled to distant
lands to find places to live. Many spent
years wandering about, looking for good
grazing land for their animals, living in
tents that they moved from place to place.
As time went on, people in different lands
developed different tastes in clothing,
cooking and customs, just like today. But
one thing they all had in common was the
same language.

When one particular group of wanderers
arrived at the land of Shinar, which is now
called Iraq, they decided to settle on a wide,

flat plain there. The countryside had everything the travellers could want, and they liked it so much that they decided they would never move on again. The travellers thought hard and came up with a big, bold plan. Instead of living in tents, they would build a lasting home for themselves – a fixed settlement made out of bricks.

They worked out how to make bricks from mud, which they could bake hard and stick together with tar. But the people didn't want to build just a village or a town, they didn't even want to build a city. They wanted to build the grandest, most beautiful city with a tower for a showpiece. A tower so tall that its top would touch the clouds. The settlers wanted news of their magnificent tower and spectacular city to spread far and wide, so they would become known throughout the world. Dreaming of fame and fortune, they began to build.

With all the digging, moulding, baking, hammering and chiselling that was going on, it wasn't long before God noticed what the people of Shinar were doing. He looked down from Heaven and was amazed at the pleasing streets that were being laid out, the stylish houses that were taking shape and the stunning tower that was soaring upwards into the sky. "My goodness!" God said to Himself. "I can't believe what these people are achieving! They're doing a wonderful job." But then a thought struck Him. "Hmmm… the only thing is, they're doing it because they want to be more important than everyone else. If I let them continue like this, they'll get quite carried away. Soon they'll want everything they have to be the biggest and best. I'd better put a stop to it before things get out of hand."

All at once, God gave the people different languages. Suddenly, they all found that they couldn't understand a word each other was saying. Without being able to communicate, their building plans ground to a halt. They couldn't work together to finish the city, which came to be known as Babel, or Babylon, because of the babble of voices inside it. Gradually everyone left Shinar in frustration and went their separate ways, seeking new homes.

From then on, as they settled in distant lands, people in different countries have spoken different languages.

Genesis chapter 11

Abram's Journey

One of the descendants of Noah's son Shem was a man called Abram. He grew up in a city called Ur, near the Persian Gulf. After Abram married he took his wife, Sarai, his father, Terah, and his orphaned nephew, Lot (whom he had brought up as his own son) to live in a northern city called

Haran. Both Ur and Haran were bustling places full of wealthy people just like Abram, who was a successful businessman. But one day, out of the blue, Abram heard God calling him.

"Abram, I want you to leave and go to the country that I will show you. I am going to make you the father of a great race of people."

It must have taken a lot of faith to do as God asked. Abram sold most of his possessions, packed up the rest and set off with his wife on a long journey without

48

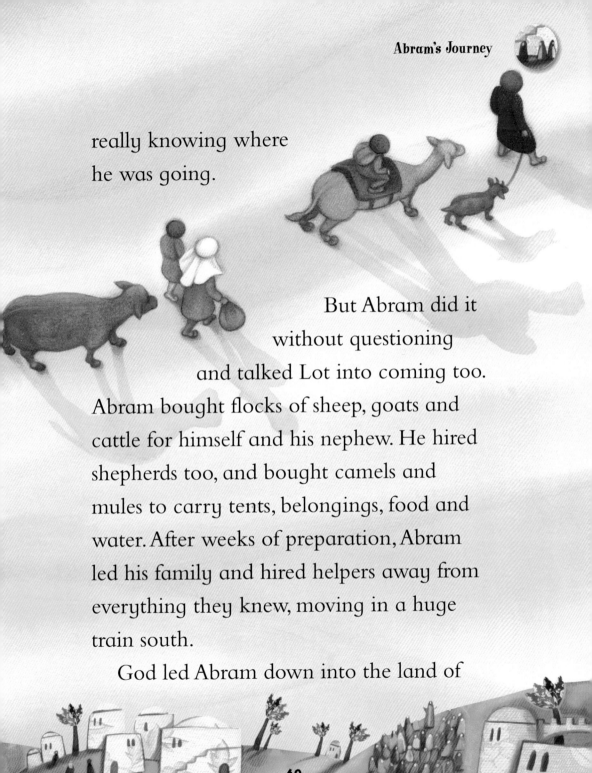

really knowing where
he was going.

But Abram did it
without questioning
and talked Lot into coming too.
Abram bought flocks of sheep, goats and
cattle for himself and his nephew. He hired
shepherds too, and bought camels and
mules to carry tents, belongings, food and
water. After weeks of preparation, Abram
led his family and hired helpers away from
everything they knew, moving in a huge
train south.

God led Abram down into the land of

Canaan, which is now called Israel. When
Abram reached a holy place called
Shechem, he heard God's voice saying,
"This is the country that I am going to give
to your descendants." Descendants! Abram
was mystified. He and his wife Sarai were
well past middle-age and although they
had always longed for a family, they had
never been able to have children. Again,
Abram tried not to question God, but to
trust once more.

They could not stay in Canaan as there
was a terrible famine, so God guided the
family through the desert to the lush land of
Egypt. Here, food and water were plentiful
but Abram found himself in quite another
kind of trouble. Pharaoh, the king of Egypt,

ordered that Sarai had to become one of his
wives. So God sent a terrible disease to
strike Pharaoh and his advisors until he
changed his mind, and he soon let Sarai go.

After that, Abram left Egypt behind and
headed north into Canaan again to a place
called Bethel. There wasn't enough
grassland for all the animals to graze on,
and Abram's and Lot's shepherds began
quarrelling and fighting over it. There was
only one thing for it – the two men split up.
Lot went east into Jordan where he settled
at a city called Sodom, while his uncle
unpacked his tents and stayed in the
countryside of Canaan. After Lot had left,
God spoke to Abram again and repeated his
vow. "Look around you," He said. "All this

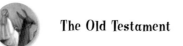

land as far as the eye can see will belong to
you and your family forever."

And so Abram waited… and waited…
Seasons came and went, but there was still
no sign that he and Sarai would ever have
children.

Over the years, God spoke to him several
times, repeating his promise. It was always
when Abram least expected it. One night,
Abram was sitting outside his tent as usual
when he heard God say, "Look up. You will
have as many descendants as there are stars
in the sky." Another time, after Abram had
made an offering to God, he had a
terrifyingly real dream. In it God walked
right next to him, vowing again that he
would have a vast, wealthy family and that

all the land from the River Nile to the River Euphrates would be theirs.

As time went on, Sarai grew concerned that she would never be able to give Abram a child so she encouraged her eighty-six-year-old husband to have a baby with her maid Hagar, instead. Hagar and Abram had a son called Ishmael, but rather than cheering Sarai up, it plunged her into sadness.

Abram turned ninety-nine years old and Sarai reached ninety, and still they had no child of their own. However God insisted that His promise remained true. "I want you and your wife to change your names as a sign of my vow," He said. "From now on, you will not be Abram and Sarai, but

Abraham and Sarah. Do what I say and trust me, and everything I have told you will come true. You and Sarah will have your own baby next year, you'll see. I want you to call him Isaac."

So Abraham and Sarah continued to wait.

Genesis chapters 11 to 13, 15 to 17

Cities of Sin

Late one morning Abraham noticed three strangers coming towards his tents. He knew, without being sure how, that they had come from Heaven. He hurried to invite them in to eat, asking Sarah to cook a special meal. Over the meal, the tallest stranger made an announcement that took

Abraham's breath away. "In nine months time I will return and Sarah will have a son." How the stranger could know what God had promised them, Abraham and Sarah had no idea.

When the strangers were ready to go, Abraham took them to a viewpoint where they could see the cities of Sodom and Gomorrah on the plain below. Abraham showed them the road to the nearest city, Sodom, telling them to go and find his nephew, Lot. Two of the strangers set off, but the tallest stayed with Abraham. All at once, Abraham knew who he was – it was God Himself in disguise! His two companions were angels.

"Abraham," said God, "Sodom and

Gomorrah are sinful cities full of wicked people. I am going to destroy them both."

"Surely there must be some good people there!" Abraham cried in horror, thinking of Lot and his family. "Please, God, promise me if your angels find just ten good people in Sodom, you'll change your mind."

"Very well," God sighed. "But only because it is you who is asking."

God's two angels arrived in Sodom that evening and went to stay the night at Lot's house. Like Abraham, Lot made his guests feel welcome by laying on a great feast. But as darkness fell, the criminals of Sodom took to the streets. Men who had noticed the two strangers arrive gathered around the house. They threw stones at the windows, trying to get the strangers to come outside so they could attack them.

Lot was outraged and stormed outside, slamming the door. "Go away!" he cried. "These men are my guests!"

The furious mob surged forwards, ready to trample Lot and break into his house. But suddenly their bloodthirsty yells turned to cries for help. They began stumbling around, tripping over each other.

The door opened and the two angels pulled Lot inside. "We have struck everyone blind," they explained.

Then the angels told Lot that God had decided to destroy Sodom and Gomorrah. "You must be gone by dawn," they warned, "so pack up your most important possessions. And as you escape the city, whatever happens, don't look behind you."

As daybreak drew near, the two angels hurried Abraham's nephew with his wife and two daughters off into the countryside. "Run!" they urged. "Don't stop until you're hiding in the hills. And remember – don't look back."

Lot and his family raced off, stumbling over stones and gasping for breath. As the sun began to rise, all of a sudden the earth shook. An ear-splitting rumbling filled the air and fire and burning stones rained down on Sodom and Gomorrah. Lot and his family ran for their lives. But Lot's wife felt the terrible heat behind them and turned round to have a look. At once she was turned into a pillar of salt.

Next morning, Abraham rose early and went to look over the plain. Where once two cities had stood, there was nothing but smouldering ruins sending up thick, black smoke.

Genesis chapters 18, 19

God's Promise Comes True

At long last, when Abraham was one hundred years old, Sarah had a baby boy whom they called Isaac. Everything had come to pass just as God had said.

The couple were so overjoyed that they thought nothing could spoil their happiness. But gradually, Sarah became eaten up with

envy of Abraham's other son, Ishmael,
whom he had with Sarah's maid, Hagar.

There had been trouble between the two
women ever since Hagar had become
pregnant. Because she was carrying
Abraham's baby, Hagar had put on airs and
graces and looked down on her
mistress. Sarah had become so
annoyed that she had treated
Hagar badly. So badly that
Hagar had eventually run
away. An angel found
Hagar weeping by a desert
spring and comforted
her, convincing her to
return. God reassured Sarah too. He said
that He would make Abraham and Hagar's

son, Ishmael, the founder of a great race. But when Abraham and Sarah had a son, Isaac, it would be his descendants who would be God's own special people.

However when Isaac was born, the rivalry Sarah felt towards Hagar brewed again. Ishmael was about fourteen and he was fond of his little brother, but Sarah hated seeing them together. She couldn't stand to be reminded that because both boys had the same father, her maid's son was equally important.

"Get rid of them!" Sarah begged Abraham. "I don't want Ishmael around, taking what should rightfully be Isaac's."

Abraham was upset because he loved both his sons. He asked God what to do.

"Don't worry," God reassured him. "Do as Sarah suggests. I'll look after Hagar and Ishmael. Trust me."

Next morning, Abraham told Hagar that she and Ishmael had to leave. With a heavy heart, he gave them food and a waterskin, and turned them out into the desert.

God kept His word and looked after Abraham's first son and his mother as they struggled to survive on their own. Once, when they were close to dying of thirst, God sent an angel to them with water. God stayed at Ishmael's side as he grew up, and he became strong and brave. Just as God had promised, He made Ishmael the founder of a great nation – the Arabs.

Genesis chapters 16, 17

A Terrible Test
for Abraham

G od had put Abraham through two
very difficult tests – having to journey
into the unknown and having to wait for so
long for he and Sarah to have a child. But
the hardest test was yet to come. When their
beloved son Isaac was about eleven years
old, God delivered Abraham some

shattering news.

"I want you to take your son to Moriah, to a place that I will show you," God told Abraham, "and offer me a sacrifice. I don't want you to kill and burn a goat or a lamb as usual, I want you to sacrifice Isaac."

Abraham was appalled. But God had spoken clearly and Abraham was quite sure what He wanted. Next morning, with agony in his heart, Abraham organized two servants to make ready to go, with firewood and provisions packed onto a donkey.

Abraham told Isaac they were going on a trip, and they set off into the desert.

For two days, Abraham walked closer to the place where he was to perform the terrible deed. Then, on the third day of travelling, they came to the foot of a hill and Abraham knew it was the place God meant. "You stay here with the donkey," Abraham told the servants. "I'm going up the hill with Isaac to pray and make an offering to God."

Isaac hurried to help, unloading the donkey and lifting up the heavy bundle of wood they would need to burn the sacrifice. Abraham carried a sharp knife and a pot of red-hot coals for starting the fire.

Then the old man and his son began

climbing, higher and higher, until they could no longer see the servants waiting below. At last they came to a little clearing and Abraham stopped and said in a strange, tense voice, "Here's the spot."

"Father, we've got the wood and coals to light the fire, but we've forgotten to bring an animal to sacrifice," pointed out Isaac.

Abraham couldn't bring himself to meet his son's eyes. "God will give us the animal," he said, his voice cracking with sorrow.

Then the two worked side by side to make an altar from stones and they arranged the firewood on top of it. Finally, the time had come for Abraham to do the unthinkable.

Imagine Isaac's terror when his father

tied him up and lifted him onto the wood, realizing that HE was to be the sacrifice.

In anguish, Abraham raised his knife high and took a deep breath, steeling himself to kill his own son, whom he loved so much.

Just as he was about to plunge the blade downwards – "STOP!" boomed a voice from Heaven into Abraham's mind. Abraham knew it was an angel speaking. "You have proved that you love God perfectly by showing you were ready to sacrifice your son, just because He said so. That is enough – do not harm Isaac."

Abraham dropped the knife. His shaking hands could hardly untie the rope that bound Isaac. Weeping so hard he thought his chest would burst, he held his beloved son and asked for his forgiveness.

Through his tears, Abraham caught sight of a nearby bush shaking – a ram was caught in it. "You see, Isaac. I told you that God would give us an animal for the sacrifice!" Abraham went over and caught the ram and offered it in Isaac's place.

When Abraham and his son had finished praying, they walked down the hill and returned home together.

Genesis chapter 22

A Tale of Twin Brothers

Isaac's mother, Sarah, lived to be one hundred and twenty-seven years old, while his father, Abraham, lived to one hundred and seventy-five. By the time they both died, Isaac had married a girl called Rebecca, from Abraham's old town of Haran. Isaac inherited his father's farming business and stayed in Canaan, following God's will just as Abraham had done.

Like Isaac's father and mother, he and Rebecca had to wait a long time before God sent them children – twenty years. It was worth the wait, for when Rebecca finally found herself expecting a baby it was not one, but two – twins! A short time before they were born, God told Rebecca, "You are having two sons, who will lead two peoples. One boy will be stronger than the other and the older one will serve the younger one." At the birth, a very strange thing happened. The second baby came out holding the first one's heel, as though he wanted to pull his older brother back and overtake. Isaac and Rebecca called the

elder boy Esau, because the
name means 'hairy' and Esau
was dark and had lots of
hair. They named
their younger, fairer
son Jacob, which
means 'someone who
wants to seize somebody
else's place'.

Time passed and the twins grew very
different in personality as well as looks.
Jacob was quiet and thoughtful. He loved
spending time at home with his mother in
the kitchen, and they became very close.
However, Esau was strong and brave. He
loved roaming around outside and he
became an excellent hunter. Esau was his

father's favourite son.

Whenever Jacob saw his father and brother together, talking and laughing in easy companionship, he couldn't help but wish that he was loved best by Isaac instead. To make matters worse, because Esau had been born before Jacob, the law said that Esau was to be given all of their father's wealth when he died. This was called his birthright. Jacob knew that he was cleverer than Esau and better suited to running his father's business. He couldn't stand to think that it was Esau's birthright to take it over eventually.

One day, Jacob was in the kitchen cooking a delicious bean stew when Esau arrived back from a hunt. "Ooooh, what's that? I'm STARVING!" he exclaimed, bending over the cooking pot and breathing in the aroma. "Can I have some now?" he begged.

Jacob's eyes glinted with a sudden idea. "I'll give you some stew," he replied, "if you promise to give me all your rights as the firstborn son."

"Done!" agreed Esau. All he could think about was his rumbling stomach, burning with hunger. "If I don't get anything to eat within the next five minutes I'll fall over and die anyway, so what use would my birthright be then?" he joked.

But Jacob was quite serious. "Say you solemnly swear," he insisted.

"I solemnly swear," promised Esau. "Now come on, give me that stew!"

Jacob ladled some stew into a bowl and gave Esau some soft, baked bread, and both twins sat back, highly pleased.

Twenty years passed and Isaac was an old, blind man who knew he didn't have long to live. One of Isaac's last wishes was for Esau to go hunting for meat for his favourite meal. Afterwards, Isaac was going to give his eldest son the blessing that officially gave him his birthright. Esau gladly set off with his bow and arrows at once.

But Rebecca had overheard. All at once, a plan came to her to trick her husband into giving her favourite son Jacob the blessing instead! First, she quickly cooked the meal her husband had asked for. Then she hurriedly dressed Jacob in Esau's clothes, so he would smell like his brother, and wrapped goatskin round his arms and neck so he would feel hairy like his brother too.

"But- But- " protested Jacob.

"I'll take the blame," Rebecca reassured her son, and sent him in with the food to see his father.

The trick worked perfectly. Isaac was at first suspicious because his tasty dinner had arrived so quickly, but Jacob said that God had helped him in his hunting. Jacob copied Esau's voice and, of course, he smelled and felt like his brother too. Isaac was fooled

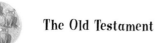

into thinking that Jacob was Esau, and gave him the all-important birthright blessing.

When Esau arrived back from the hunt and went to his father, they both quickly realized they had been tricked. How they wept with frustration and regret. However it was too late, the old man could not take back his blessing.

Later, in private, Esau began to feel angry. "I'll wait until father dies," he swore to himself, "but no longer than that. Then I shall have my revenge on Jacob."

Genesis chapters 25 to 28

Jacob's Dream

Jacob had won his twin brother Esau's birthright, but his joy soon melted into shame and regret. His old, blind father was so bitterly disappointed that he could hardly talk to Jacob, and Esau couldn't stand the sight of him either. It was only because Esau didn't want to upset his father even further that he hadn't already battered his smaller, weaker twin brother. Only Jacob's mother still loved him – and now he was about to lose her too. Rebecca was so worried about what Esau would do to her favourite son once Isaac died, that she told Jacob he had no choice but to leave. "You must go far away, well out of Esau's reach," Rebecca urged. "Hurry to my brother, your Uncle Laban, in the city of Haran. You'll be safe there. We'll just have to hope that your brother cools down and forgives you, so you can come back."

So Jacob left his home and his family in disgrace, with no one for company and no possessions for comfort. He set off for Haran through the desert, wondering why he had done what he had done. At the end of the first lonely day's travelling, Jacob came across a rocky, sheltered spot where he could camp for the night. Weary and miserable, Jacob found a flattish, smooth stone that would have to do as a pillow and laid down to try to get some rest.

Alone in the desert, hungry, cold and worried about wild animals, Jacob did not sleep well. He tossed and turned for hours, and when he did eventually fall asleep he had a very strange dream.

Jacob dreamt that a blinding light suddenly burst from the dark night sky. He shielded his eyes and blinked until he got used to the glare and could open them properly. Then Jacob saw that the light shone in a steady, sloping beam down to the ground. People in bright, shimmering clothes were gliding up and down. With a shock, Jacob realized that he was looking at a staircase from Heaven to Earth and that the people were angels. Suddenly he felt God Himself standing beside him. "Yes, I am the Lord," said God. "And as I promised your grandfather Abraham and your father Isaac, I am going to give the land on which you are lying to you and your family. You will have as many descendants as there are specks of dust on the ground. Now remember, you will never be alone. I will always be with you. I will look after you, and wherever you go, I will make sure that one day you

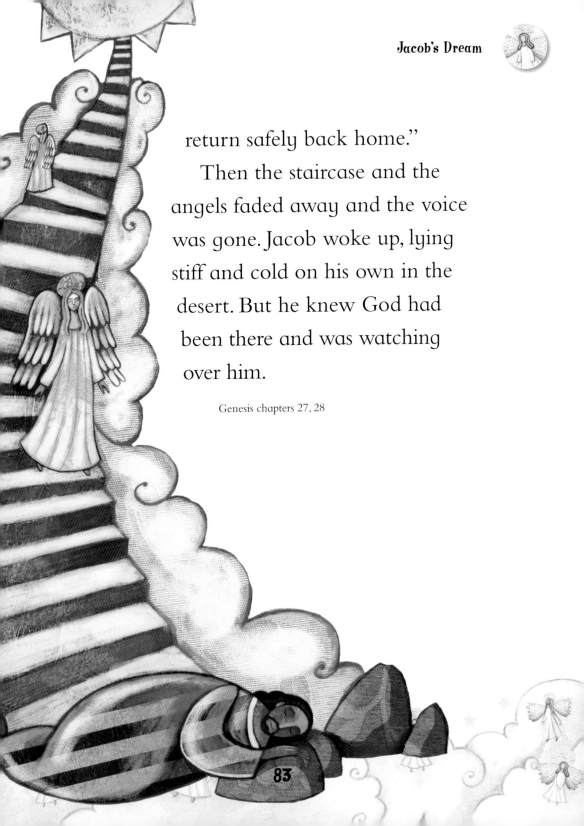

return safely back home."

Then the staircase and the angels faded away and the voice was gone. Jacob woke up, lying stiff and cold on his own in the desert. But he knew God had been there and was watching over him.

Genesis chapters 27, 28

Jacob the Trickster is Tricked!

After weeks of travelling, there came a day when Jacob felt sure he must be near his destination of Haran. He stopped at a well where shepherds were watering their flocks and asked if he was far away.

"Yes, you are indeed at Haran," the shepherds replied.

"Do you know Laban?" Jacob asked.

"Of course!" the shepherds told him.
"Everyone around here knows Laban. In
fact his daughter, Rachel, should be coming
to water his sheep around now. Wait a while
and you'll catch her."

So Jacob sat down and waited. Sure
enough, a few minutes later there came the
baaing of sheep and the clanking of sheep
bells. A flock arrived driven by the most
beautiful girl he had ever seen. It was love
at first sight.

Jacob hurried to lift away the heavy, flat
stone that covered the well and help water
the sheep. "You must be Rachel," he said,
rather shyly. "You don't know me, but I am
your cousin, Jacob."

85

Rachel was delighted and ran to tell her father that they had a visitor. Laban hurried to greet his nephew. He welcomed him into his house, where he introduced Jacob to his elder daughter, Leah, too.

After resting for a while and eating, the time came for Jacob to confess the shameful reason why he had come to visit. But it didn't make any difference to Laban.

"Of course you must stay with me, you're family," his uncle cried. "Make yourself at home."

So Jacob did. He tried to show his thanks to his uncle by working hard at whatever Laban asked. Jacob put so much effort into everything he did that, after a month, Laban began to feel guilty that he wasn't paying him as he was paying his other workers.

"Uncle, lodging and food are more than enough," Jacob explained. "I wouldn't dream of taking any money."

"Even if you won't take money, you must let me give you something for your labours," Laban insisted. "Now Jacob, tell me what you would like."

Then Jacob saw a fantastic opportunity. "I'll work for you for nothing for seven years," he said, "if you will then give me your daughter Rachel as my wife."

Laban was a little taken aback, but after a moment's thought he grinned. "I can't think of anyone else I'd rather see as Rachel's husband," he said. The two men shook hands and the deal was done.

So Jacob toiled for Laban for seven years. He loved Rachel so much that just being near her made the months speed by.

At last the time came for Jacob to claim his reward. His uncle called his family and friends together for a great marriage feast. However Laban was cunning like his sister, Jacob's mother. He played a trick on Jacob – in the darkness of the wedding night, he sent his elder daughter Leah to Jacob instead of Rachel.

In the morning, when Jacob realized he had been fooled into marrying the wrong daughter, he was devastated. His uncle just shrugged. "It's the custom in this country for the elder daughter to marry first," he stated.

"But I'll give you Rachel to be your second wife as long as you promise to work for me for another seven years."

Jacob didn't have a choice. He had to wait until the end of the week, when the celebrations for his marriage to Leah were over. Then he married his beloved Rachel. Labouring for Laban for a further seven years was a small price to pay for finally getting the woman he loved.

Genesis chapter 29

Jacob Makes Amends

Jacob was a very skilled farmer. With him in charge, his Uncle Laban's flocks and herds grew several times bigger and the sheep, cattle and goats were fatter and finer than ever. Jacob stayed longer than the fourteen years he had promised, and built up stocks of animals for himself. Eventually he became even wealthier than his uncle. Finally Jacob decided that enough was enough, he wanted to return home. He told his wives and they ordered the servants to pack everything up and prepare the animals. They all set off in a long train across the countryside.

As Jacob drew closer to Canaan, he became more and more worried. After all, when he left, his brother Esau had been determined to kill him! Jacob sent messengers galloping ahead, to tell Esau that he was coming and that he wanted to make amends. But he was worried to see his messengers returning so soon. "Sir," they panted, "your brother is heading this way with a force of four hundred men!"

"Then Esau must have made up his mind to attack me," Jacob told himself in deep dismay. He ordered his herders to count out two hundred and twenty goats, two hundred and twenty sheep, thirty camels and their young, forty cows, ten bulls and thirty donkeys. "Keep all the animals separate," Jacob instructed the herders. "Drive every group forward an hour apart and when you each reach Esau, tell him that the animals are a present from me." Jacob thought that perhaps by the time he sees Esau, he may have forgiven him.

That evening Jacob camped on his own. He knew it might be his last night. As darkness drew in, he lay awake thinking everything over.

Suddenly, from nowhere, a man jumped on Jacob and began to attack him. Stunned, Jacob fought for his life, but the stranger didn't give in. They wrestled for hours, until finally – CRACK! Jacob collapsed in agony as one of the stranger's blows put his hip out of joint.

"I am the Lord," the stranger announced, and Jacob was stunned to realize that it was God Himself. "You have done well," God continued. "You have won

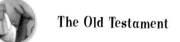

your struggles with others and now I
say you have won your struggle
with me too. I want you to change
your name. From now on,
everyone should call you Israel."

The sun rose and God was
gone, and Jacob hobbled away
to rejoin his family.

It wasn't long before Esau
and his four hundred men
arrived in a cloud of dust.
Jacob told his family to
stay well back and
limped forward all alone
to face his brother. Esau jumped off
his horse and ran forwards, and Jacob sank
to his knees before his brother, bowing low

in the dirt. But Esau hurried to help him up, throwing his arms around Jacob, kissing him, and both the brothers began to weep.

"Welcome, my long-lost brother," Esau sobbed. "Welcome to you and your family."

And Jacob was overjoyed to be home at last.

Genesis chapters 30 to 33

Joseph the Dreamer

Jacob was one of the wealthiest men in Canaan. He had vast herds of cattle, sheep, goats, camels and donkeys, and he owned many tents, filled with possessions. However the thing he held most dear was Joseph, his eleventh son. Joseph's mother was Jacob's true love, Rachel. The couple had waited for many years before God sent them a child. So long that Jacob had ten sons by three other wives by then. So Joseph was very special.

Unfortunately, Jacob made it obvious that Joseph was his favourite. He sometimes kept Joseph at home with him while his other sons went into the fields on farming duties. Of course this made Jacob's other sons resentful of their brother. Even more so when Joseph turned seventeen. Jacob had an expensive coat made for him. It was a

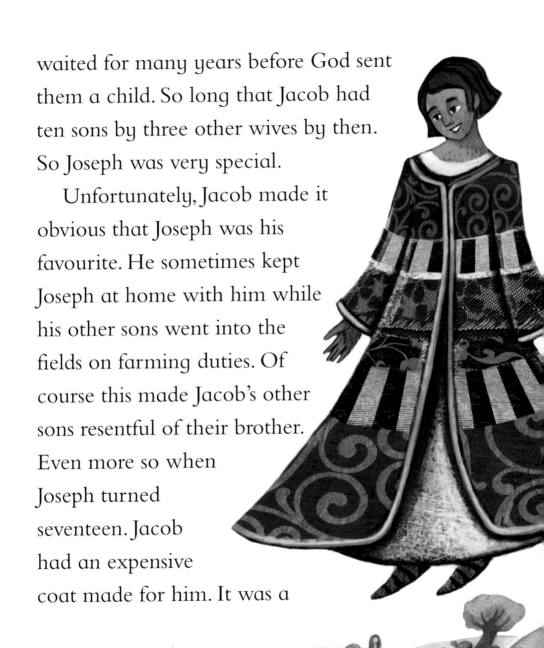

beautiful, long coat with big sleeves, richly sewn with many different colours. It drove Jacob's other sons wild with jealousy.

The situation went from bad to worse when Joseph began to have strange dreams.

"Guess what?" he asked his brothers one morning. "Last night, I dreamt that we were in the fields at harvest time tying the wheat into sheaves, when my sheaf stood up straight. Then your sheaves gathered around it and bowed to mine!"

"Who do you think you are?" spat one of the brothers.

"Do you see yourself as better than us?" growled another.

"Do you think you're going to be a king and rule over us?" scowled a third.

A little while later, Joseph had another odd dream and again made the mistake of telling his brothers about it.

"I dreamt last night that I saw the sun, the moon and eleven stars all bowing down to me." The brothers knew that Joseph meant that their father, mother and the eleven of them were like his servants. How furious they were!

One day, when Jacob had kept Joseph at home with him and sent his other sons out to work, he decided to send Joseph to check on them. Out in the hot fields, the tired, thirsty brothers saw him coming, fresh from home, all dressed up in his fancy coat and they had a terrible idea.

"Here comes the dreamer!" one of them

laughed. "I wish we could get rid of him once and for all."

"Well, this is our chance," another noticed.

"There's no one around, it's the perfect opportunity!" a third brother agreed.

"Let's kill him and throw the body into that pit over there," another brother urged.

"We could tell our father that he was attacked by wild animals!" one lad suggested.

"Stop it!" cried the eldest brother, Reuben, horrified. "We can't kill Joseph! Do you really want his blood on your hands?" he pointed out. "If you must, throw him into that old, dry well over there and leave him – but don't murder him!" (Little did the brothers know that once they'd all gone home, Reuben intended to sneak off back to the well and rescue Joseph).

And that's what the brothers did. They fell on Joseph, ripping off his special coat, and then lowered him into the dried-up well, taking away the rope.

Pleased with themselves, the brothers ignored Joseph's cries for help, and sat down to eat – all except Reuben. He didn't feel like joining them. He stomped off on his own to see to the animals in the furthest pastures.

While Reuben was gone, a camel train of spice traders came passing by on their way to Egypt. One of the brothers, Judah, had another awful idea. "Reuben was right. We shouldn't harm Joseph – he is our flesh and blood, after all," he announced, with a glint in his eye. "I have a better plan – we'll sell him instead. I'm sure the traders will pay a good price for a slave."

By the time Reuben returned, Judah and the brothers had accepted twenty pieces of silver from the traders and Joseph was gone.

"What have you done?" Reuben cried. "Shame on you, Judah. Shame on you all! Now what are you going to tell Father?"

In desperation, the brothers came up

with a final part to their wicked plan. They killed a young goat, dipped Joseph's torn coat in its blood and took it home to show their father. "Joseph was killed and eaten by wild animals," they explained to Jacob.

The old man collapsed in sorrow, weeping and mourning for his beloved Joseph. "I will grieve for my son until the day I die," he sobbed.

Genesis chapter 37

A Slave in Egypt

Sold by his family, marched by strangers all the way to a foreign land, and then traded in the market place as a slave – Joseph was exhausted and terrified. Yet his strong character must have shone through because the man who bought Joseph trusted him to work in his house, not in his fields or as a labourer. The man was very important and wealthy. His name was Potiphar and he was captain of the soldiers who guarded Pharaoh, the king of Egypt. God stayed with Joseph all the time and cheered him up, helping him do his duties well. Potiphar was so pleased that he kept promoting Joseph. After a while, Joseph was running Potiphar's whole household.

Now Joseph was not only hard-working and trustworthy, he was also quite handsome. So much so that Potiphar's wife fell in love with him. Each day, she seized every opportunity behind her husband's back to flirt with Joseph, trying to tempt him into having an affair. Joseph was loyal to Potiphar and kept turning her down. But

Potiphar's wife was determined to get what she wanted. One day, she lay in wait for Joseph and grabbed him by his cloak. Joseph had to wriggle out of it in order to escape her clutches and run off! Then the scorned woman saw a way to get her own back. She put on a show of being deeply upset and accused Joseph of having forced his way into her bedroom. She said that when she screamed out, he had ran away, leaving only his cloak behind.

Of course, Potiphar was furious. He had Joseph flung into prison.

Joseph could have wept and wailed. He could have despaired and died, but God stayed with him and lifted his spirits. The jailer was fond of the reliable, capable young man and began giving him special jobs. Soon, he put Joseph in charge of all the other prisoners.

Two of the prisoners in Joseph's care were Pharaoh's butler and baker. One morning, Joseph found them looking anxious because they had both had strange dreams that they couldn't understand.

"Tell me about them," Joseph urged. "Maybe God will explain to me what they're about."

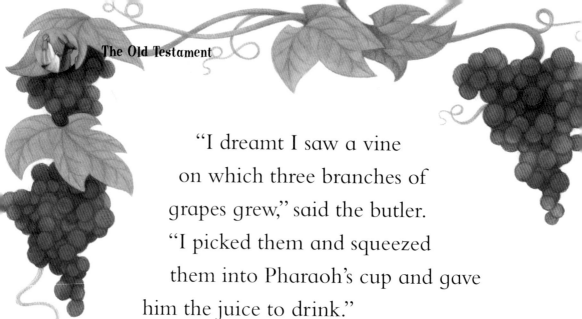

"I dreamt I saw a vine
on which three branches of
grapes grew," said the butler.
"I picked them and squeezed
them into Pharaoh's cup and gave
him the juice to drink."

Joseph felt sure he knew what the
dream meant, thanks to God. "In three
days' time Pharaoh is going to pardon you
and give you your job back," he explained.

The butler was delighted. "Oh thank
you! Thank you so much!" he cried.

"My friend," Joseph said, "just promise
me that when you're released, you won't
forget about me. Please tell Pharaoh about
me and beg him to release me, for I don't
deserve to be in here!"

"Well, what about my dream?" asked the baker excitedly. "I dreamt I was carrying three baskets of white bread on my head, and the birds were eating the bread out of the top basket."

Joseph's face fell as the meaning came to him. "I hate to tell you this," he said sadly, "but in three days' time, Pharaoh is going to hang you."

The dreams came true. In three days' time, the baker was put to death, while the butler was released and set back to work for Pharaoh. He was so joyful that any thoughts of Joseph went out of his head. Joseph remained in prison, quite forgotten.

Genesis chapters 39, 40

The Ruler
of Egypt

One morning, there was a commotion in the royal palace of Egypt. Pharaoh had awoken deeply troubled. He had had two strange dreams, which he was sure meant something but he had no idea what. In the first dream, Pharaoh had been standing by the River Nile. Seven fat cows

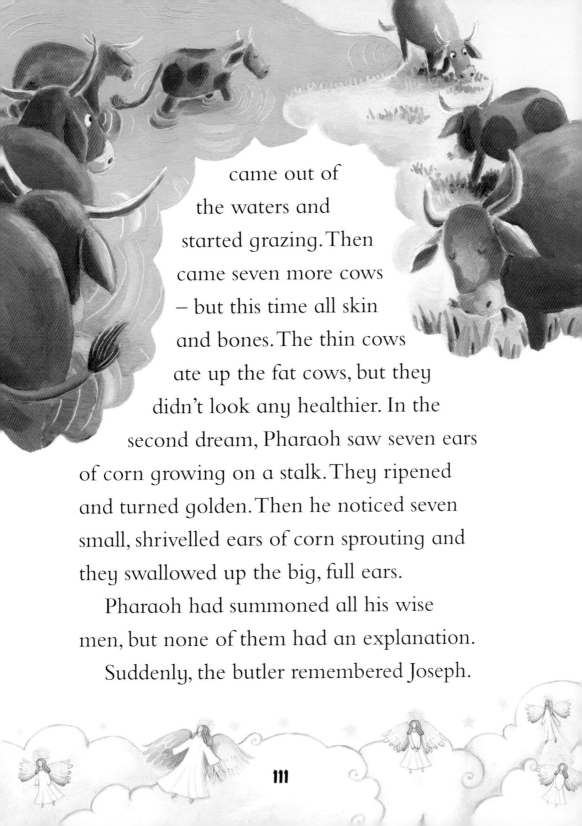

came out of
the waters and
started grazing. Then
came seven more cows
– but this time all skin
and bones. The thin cows
ate up the fat cows, but they
didn't look any healthier. In the
second dream, Pharaoh saw seven ears
of corn growing on a stalk. They ripened
and turned golden. Then he noticed seven
small, shrivelled ears of corn sprouting and
they swallowed up the big, full ears.

Pharaoh had summoned all his wise
men, but none of them had an explanation.
Suddenly, the butler remembered Joseph.

Two years had passed and he wasn't even sure if Joseph was still alive. But now he told Pharaoh all about the amazing young Israelite man locked in the dungeon.

Pharaoh sent for him at once. Joseph was hauled out of prison and brought into the magnificent courtroom of the great King of Egypt. Then Pharaoh described his dreams and Joseph felt God give him the interpretation.

"Both dreams mean the same," Joseph announced to the anxiously waiting king. "For the next seven years, Egypt will have excellent harvests. But during the following seven years the crops will fail and there will be a terrible famine. Here's what God says to do. Hire a minister with officials under him to take charge of your kingdom. For the next seven years, they should collect one-fifth of all the grain that is grown and store it away in warehouses. During the seven years of famine, you can share out the grain so your people don't starve."

"Really?" said Pharaoh. "Is that what your God thinks?" He thought for a while and everyone in the courtroom held their breath to see whether the king was pleased.

Pharaoh descended from his gleaming throne and approached Joseph. He took a huge gold ring off his finger and gave it to the former prisoner. "You will be the minister," he ordered. "I can't think of anyone better. You start straight away."

Genesis chapter 41

The Silver Cup

Joseph was now thirty years old, and
Pharaoh's right-hand man. He had
more power in Egypt than anyone, except
the king himself.

Seven years passed. Then, as predicted,
the crops failed, and not just in Egypt but
in all the countries nearby. Fortunately,

Joseph had made sure that the Egyptian
warehouses were fully stocked. And as
news of the stores spread, starving people
came from far and wide to ask for food.

Among them were Joseph's brothers
from Canaan. Joseph's father, Jacob, only
sent ten of his sons to Egypt to buy grain.
After losing Joseph he couldn't bear to part
with his and Rachel's only other son,
Benjamin, so he had kept him at home.

More than twenty years had passed
since the brothers had sold Joseph into
slavery. Joseph was now married to an
Egyptian. He acted like an Egyptian. He
looked like a magnificent Egyptian prince.
He even spoke Egyptian. So of course,
when the brothers were called into his

presence to buy grain, they didn't
recognize him, but Joseph knew who they
were. He was disappointed that Benjamin
– his favourite brother – wasn't with them,
so Joseph decided to trick them in order to
get to see him.

"I don't believe you have come to ask
for grain," Joseph told his brothers through
an interpreter. "I think you are spies!"

"We're not spies, we're brothers!" they
protested. "We were twelve, but one died
long ago and the youngest of us is at

home with our father."

"Then prove it," Joseph ordered. "One of you must journey back and fetch your youngest brother. I'll give you some time to think about who is going to go." And he had them all thrown in prison.

After three days, Joseph ordered the brothers to be brought in front of him again.

"I've decided to let you return home with the grain you need," he announced. "But you must still bring me your youngest brother and to make sure you do, I shall keep one of you here as hostage."

He clapped his hands and at once, his servants grabbed Simeon, tying him up and taking him away.

It was with heavy hearts that the nine brothers set off to Canaan. They were even more dismayed when they discovered that the money they had paid for the grain was somehow in their sacks. "What's happened?" they wondered, "This is going to land us in deeper trouble." They had no idea that Joseph had ordered his servants to put the money there as another trick.

When they told Jacob that they had to return to Egypt with Benjamin, the anguished old man cried, "No! No way! I've lost Joseph, and now Simeon has gone. I'm not letting Benjamin out of my sight!"

But the weeks went by and the famine grew worse and eventually the Egyptian corn was used up. Jacob had no choice but to send his sons back to buy more – this time with Benjamin. The grief-stricken old man loaded them down with expensive gifts for the powerful Egyptian minister in the hope that he would be pleased and allow all ten of his sons to return.

As soon as Joseph heard that his brothers had arrived back in Egypt, he ordered them to be brought to the palace. The men were terrified they were going to be arrested for taking the money they had found in their sacks. "It was a mistake," they told Joseph's steward, giving it back. "Look – it's all here, count it."

But Joseph hadn't invited them to his house for that. Instead, he gave them a feast. Joseph was so delighted to see

Benjamin that he gave him five times as much to eat and drink as the others!

Next day, all ten brothers were hugely relieved to find that they were allowed to set off back to Canaan with all the grain they could carry.

However, they hadn't gone far when they heard pounding hooves behind them, and when they looked it was Joseph's steward chasing after them. He insisted on opening the brothers' sacks, from eldest to youngest, and in the last one, Benjamin's, was Joseph's best silver cup!

"Thieves!" accused the steward, knowing it was another of Joseph's tricks.

In utter despair, the brothers went with the steward back to the city and begged Joseph for forgiveness.

"Your punishment will be that Benjamin must stay here and be my slave," Joseph announced. "The rest of you are free to go."

Then Judah sprang up and pleaded, "Your Highness, our father has already lost his favourite son. If we return without this boy, he will surely die of grief. I beg you – let me stay and be your slave instead."

Then Joseph felt that his heart would break. "Everybody out!" he ordered, and his advisors left him alone with his brothers. Finally he told them who he was. "Don't blame yourselves for selling me into slavery," Joseph told the astonished men with great grace. "It was all part of God's plan for me." Then he threw his arms around Benjamin in tears, and hugged and kissed them all.

Pharaoh was delighted when he heard that Joseph had a family who were alive and well. He invited them all to live in one of the lushest parts of Egypt, where Joseph could look after them.

Jacob was reunited with his beloved son, Joseph, and lived out the last few years of his life in happiness.

Genesis chapters 41 to 46

The Baby in the Basket

Joseph and his brothers lived in Egypt for the rest of their lives and had many children, grandchildren and great-grandchildren. They did well in farming and business and became wealthy and powerful. As time passed, the Egyptians began calling them Israelites after the special name God had given to Jacob. Years went by and the number of Israelites grew, and different pharaohs came and went. After four hundred years, one king became particularly worried because there were so many Israelites. He told his advisors, "I am worried that if there was ever a war, the Israelites might turn against us and join with our enemies to defeat Egypt. We must find a way to stop their numbers growing further and to make them less powerful."

Pharaoh decided on drastic action – he sent his soldiers to seize the Israelites and turn them into slaves. Then he appointed slave-drivers to set the Israelites to work, labouring on roads and building sites, and in the fields.

But still the number of Israelites
increased, and families spread further
throughout Egypt. Furious, Pharaoh came
up with an even more wicked plan. He
ordered his soldiers to search out every
newborn Israelite boy and kill them all!

Of course, many desperate families tried
to hide their beloved babies. One woman,
who already had a daughter, Miriam, and a
son, Aaron, kept her newborn boy hidden
for three months. But as time went on, he
became bigger and noisier and harder to
conceal. In the end, the desperate woman
took a reed basket and covered it with tar
so it was watertight. She gently laid her
baby in it and took it down to the River
Nile, setting it in the thick, tall grasses at the

water's edge so it wouldn't float away. She told Miriam to stay a little way off to see that the baby was alright.

It wasn't long before the little girl saw a grand procession making its way down to the river. Her eyes opened wide at the sight of a young woman in magnificent robes, splendid jewels and rich makeup, accompanied by many servants and slaves. It was the princess, coming to bathe! The little girl watched, hardly daring to breathe, as the princess caught sight of the basket in the rushes and sent a servant to bring it to her. As soon as the princess saw the baby boy inside, she realized that he must be an Israelite. As she lifted the baby up, he began to cry and her heart melted with pity for the hungry, helpless child. She decided to take the baby home and keep him.

Bravely, Miriam dared to approach the princess, curtseying low. "Would you like me to find an Israelite nurse to look after him, Your Highness?" she suggested nervously.

The princess was pleased, and the little girl dashed home and fetched her mother!

So the little boy was at first cared for by his real mother, then given the education of an Egyptian prince. For the princess loved him so much, she adopted him as her own son. She called him Moses, which means 'to draw out', because she had rescued him by having him drawn out of the water.

Exodus chapters 1, 2

The Burning Bush

Moses was brought up as Egyptian royalty, but he knew that he was an Israelite by birth. As he grew up, he found it unbearable that he was living a rich, comfortable life of freedom, while other Israelites suffered as Egyptian slaves. One day, when he was a young man, he saw an

Egyptian guard savagely hitting an Israelite man, and something inside him snapped. Moses beat the guard off, leaving him lying dead at his feet. News of his crime quickly spread. Moses knew that even the princess would not be able to save him from a terrible punishment, perhaps even death. He had no choice but to run away.

Moses fled to a country called Midian and settled into the quiet life of a shepherd. He looked after the flocks belonging to a village priest named Jethro, and he married his daughter, Zipporah. Years came and went and Moses' former life as an Egyptian royal seemed like a dream.

One day, Moses was out with his sheep when he came upon a very strange sight.

A bush was on fire, but the leaves
and branches of the bush
weren't burning away. While
Moses marvelled, a voice
suddenly boomed,
"Moses, come no closer
to this holy place! I am
God – the God of your
fathers, Abraham, Isaac
and Jacob."

Moses fell to
the ground, covering
his face in terror.

"I have seen how my
people, the Israelites, suffer in
Egypt," echoed the voice. "But I will
free them from slavery and return them

to Canaan, a land of plenty that I promised would be their own. I want you to return to Egypt and rescue my people. Convince them to follow you and demand Pharaoh to release them."

Moses was shocked. "No one will believe that my orders are from you, Lord," he protested.

God gave Moses three magic signs so that he could prove it. Firstly, if Moses threw his shepherd's staff onto the ground, it turned into a snake! As soon as he picked it up again, it turned back into wood. Secondly, if Moses thrust his hand into his robe, it came out covered with scales and sores of the disease leprosy! When he put it back again, it was healed and healthy.

Lastly, God told Moses that if he poured some water from the River Nile onto the ground, it would turn into blood!

Moses was stunned, but even so, he was still unsure. "How can I be a leader, Lord?" he argued. "I don't even like talking in public. I go red and can't get the words out. Isn't there someone else you can send?"

"I have already told your brother Aaron to come and find you – he can do the talking," insisted God.

Moses hurried home and explained to his wife and his father-in-law what he had been ordered to do. To Moses' great surprise, Jethro believed him. God reassured Moses that it was safe for him to return to Egypt as a new pharaoh had come to the throne.

So he and his wife packed up and set off through the countryside.

As they neared Egypt, Aaron came out to meet them, just as God had promised. The long-lost brothers hurried to see the Israelite elders straight away. While Aaron explained that God had told Moses to lead the Israelites out of slavery, Moses proved that his message was from God by demonstrating the three magic signs in front of everyone. How the Israelites gasped! They believed Moses and sent up prayers of thanks that God had sent them help.

Exodus chapters 2 to 4

The Nine Plagues of Egypt

As God had ordered, Moses and Aaron requested an audience with Pharaoh himself. They were summoned to appear in Pharaoh's magnificent courtroom, in front of all his guards, advisors and magicians. "We have come at God's command to ask that you set the people of Israel free!" the brothers dared to tell Pharaoh.

But Pharaoh just laughed and waved for
Moses and Aaron to be taken away. Then
he set the Israelites even tougher tasks to do,
making their lives even harder and more
miserable.

"I've made the situation worse!" Moses
told God, but God insisted that he try again.

So once more Moses and Aaron went to
see Pharaoh. This time Aaron threw down
Moses' staff, which turned into a snake,
wriggling on the floor. Pharaoh signalled
to his magicians and they too threw their
staffs onto the floor, which also turned
into slithering snakes.

Pharaoh didn't
even care when

Aaron's snake swallowed up all of the
magicians' snakes. "Audience over," he
announced coldly.

Moses despaired, but God told him what
to do. Early the next day, Moses and Aaron
went down to the River Nile and waited for
Pharaoh to take his morning walk there.
When Pharaoh refused their demands,
Aaron hit the waters with the staff. At once,
the Nile turned to blood. The river ran red
for seven days – all the fish died and there
was no water to drink.

Yet the cold-hearted king was unmoved.

Then Moses signalled Aaron to stretch
the staff over the Nile, and millions of frogs
came hopping out of every river, stream and
pond in Egypt. Everywhere anyone looked

there were frogs… anything anyone touched had frogs on it… the people couldn't move for frogs!

Then Pharaoh sent for Moses. "Tell your god to make this stop and I will let your people go."

Immediately, there were so many dead frogs that the Egyptians had to pile them into huge, stinking heaps.

Pharaoh went back on his word.

So God ordered Moses to tell Aaron to hit the ground with the staff. The dust swirled and billions of lice swarmed out of the ground and over Egypt. Soon, everything that had been slimy with leaping frogs was itching with biting lice.

But Pharaoh's heart was as hard as stone.

So God sent vast clouds of flies
humming into Egypt. They darkened the
skies and blanketed the ground, dive
bombing people's heads, landing on their
eyelids, fluttering up their nostrils. But not
one fly entered the house of an Israelite.

Then Pharaoh summoned Moses.
"I will do as you ask," he announced, "if
your god rids us of these flies!"

Once again, as soon as the flies were
gone, Pharaoh simply broke his promise.

So God sent a dreadful disease which
wiped out every horse, camel, ox, goat
and sheep in the land – except for those
belonging to the Israelites.

Still, Pharaoh would not give in.

Then God told Moses and Aaron to take

a handful of ashes and throw it up into the air. As the wind blew the ashes across Egypt, an awful sickness spread, which caused terrible boils to break out over every person and each remaining animal – unless they were Israelite.

It just made Pharaoh more determined.

So God told Moses to stretch his staff up to the heavens… Thunder crashed, lighting flashed and hail fell from the skies in mighty torrents, flattening trees and plants. Everywhere except in the fields belonging to the Israelites.

At last Pharaoh called Moses again. "Enough!" he spat. "Make it stop and I will do what you ask." Moses prayed and the storm calmed. "I lied," announced Pharaoh triumphantly. He turned on his heel and strode away.

The very next day, a strange wind blew across Egypt, thick with locusts. Within a few hours they had eaten every blade of grass, every leaf, every ear of corn, every fruit on the trees.

"Aaaaaaargh!" howled Pharaoh. "Alright, the Israelites can go." The wind changed direction and the locusts were blown into the Red Sea and drowned.

But still, Pharaoh did not go through with his promise. So God told Moses to stretch out his hand and Egypt was swamped in total darkness for three days and nights. As his miserable people stumbled around blindly and the country ground to a

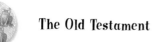

halt, Pharaoh once again summoned Moses. "The Israelites may go, and this time I will not go back on my word," he spat, his eyes full of hate. "As long as they leave all their sheep, goats, camels and donkeys.

Moses listened to God.

"No," he replied, and Pharaoh turned white with fury.

"Then get out," roared the cruel king. "Your people will be my slaves forever. If I ever lay eyes on you again, you will die!"

Exodus chapters 5 to 10

The First Passover

God spoke to Moses and said, "I am going to send one last plague upon Egypt, so terrible that Pharaoh will be glad to let the Israelites go. At midnight, every firstborn child in Egypt shall die. From the firstborn of Pharaoh to the firstborn of the lowliest servant to the firstborn of every animal. No one shall escape – unless they are an Israelite. Here's what they have to do to be spared. Every family must cook a lamb and smear their doorposts with the blood. Then I shall know which houses are Israelite homes. Forever after, this day will be called Passover and celebrated as the first day of the year. By my passing over the land tonight, my people will be set free – the beginning of a new era."

Next morning, nothing could be heard in Egypt except for wailing and screaming as people discovered their loved ones were dead. People and animals had breathed their last in every household across the land – except for the homes of the Israelites.

Once again Moses and Aaron found

themselves before Pharaoh, who was weeping over his own dead firstborn son. "Take your people and go!" he whispered. "Be gone, and never darken my lands again."

All over Pharaoh's country, the doomed Egyptians were so desperate to be rid of the Israelites that they offered them gold, silver and jewels to leave right away.

And that is how over six hundred thousand men, women and children came to gather to walk out of Egypt. After over four hundred years of captivity, the Israelites were heading home.

Exodus chapters 11, 12

Escape Across the Red Sea

God Himself guided the Israelites as they travelled out of Egypt and into the wilderness beyond. By day He appeared as a column of cloud and by night, as a column of fire, so they could follow Him.

The Israelites had reached the sands of the Red Sea when they noticed a massive cloud of dust behind them in the distance, rushing towards them at great speed.

It was the Egyptian army! The minute that Pharaoh had ordered the Israelites to leave, he regretted his decision. In a whirlwind of hatred, he called for his best armour and ordered six hundred of his finest charioteers to make ready to chase after his former slaves.

The Israelites were terrified and turned on Moses. "Did you lead us out of captivity only to meet our deaths in the desert?" they cried.

"Don't be afraid," Moses told the Israelites. "The Lord will protect you, wait and see." And God spoke to Moses, telling him what to do.

With the Egyptian army thundering
ever closer, Moses urged the Israelites
forward – straight towards the Red Sea.
Then the column of cloud blew over
Pharaoh and his charioteers, smothering
them so they couldn't see their way ahead.
While the bewildered, frustrated Egyptians
were forced to slow their pace, Moses
reached the foaming seashore and stretched
out his hand towards the ocean.

An immense wind blew up, nearly
sweeping the Israelites off their feet. It
howled and hurled, and with great gusts this
way and that it split the waves. The wind
drove the waters to the right and left, higher
and higher, until they rolled back leaving a
wide pathway of seabed in between. Then

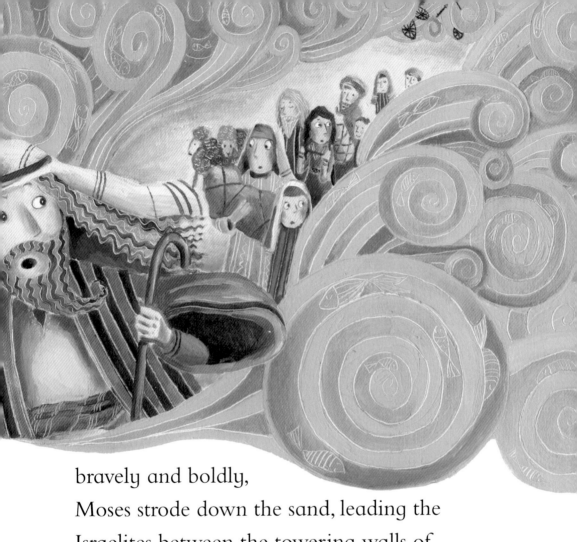

bravely and boldly,
Moses strode down the sand, leading the
Israelites between the towering walls of
water on either side.

Then came the Egyptian army,
galloping forwards. How petrified they were
when they saw the waters of the Red Sea

divided in front of them. Yet they plunged into the passage as the last of the Israelites reached the sandy shore on the other side.

As Pharaoh and his charioteers sped ever closer to the Israelites, Moses stretched out his hand once more. Then the towering walls of water teetered, toppled and crashed down. The Red Sea closed over the Egyptians, drowning each and every one, and the Israelites were truly free at last.

Exodus chapters 13, 14

Miracles in the Wilderness

How the Israelites celebrated when God saved them from the clutches of Pharaoh and the Egyptian army. Moses' and Aaron's sister, Miriam, led the women in dancing along the shores of the Red Sea, singing a song of thanks to God.

And so the Israelites trusted Moses and

believed that he was doing God's will, and followed him uncomplainingly into the desert. But after six weeks of plodding along on foot, their food began to run out. The Israelites became exhausted and hungry. People started to moan to Moses and Aaron, saying things like: "It would have been better if you'd left us in Egypt, at least then we had plenty to eat. Here, we're all going to die of starvation!"

Of course, God heard what his people were saying and reassured Moses that they would be well provided for. "Tell everyone they'll have poultry for dinner and bread for breakfast," he commanded. "Then perhaps they'll remember who I am and learn to trust me."

Moses had no idea what God had planned but he had perfect faith, so he gathered the people and told them anyway. That evening, sure enough, a flock of small birds called quails flew into the Israelites' camp, which they caught and ate. The following morning, when the night dew had lifted from the desert soil, the Israelites saw that the ground was covered with small, white flakes. They tried to eat it and found that it was delicious, it tasted of honey! The people called the flakes 'manna'. Moses told everyone they could gather as much as they could eat that same day, but some people were greedy and collected more. They hoarded it away secretly, and overnight it rotted and became full of maggots. The Israelites hadn't needed to store the manna because every morning for six days more, it appeared on the ground. On the sixth day, Moses told everyone they could collect enough for two days because no manna was going to appear on the next day, which was the seventh day – God's holy day. Yet the Sabbath came around and still some people went out searching for manna. "When will these people learn to follow my rules?" God sighed to Moses.

Days passed and as the Israelites tramped through the desert their water supplies began to run low. "Why did you bring us out of Egypt to kill us by thirst?" everyone began to complain once more. Then God told Moses to go to a certain rock and strike it with his staff. As he did so, cold water burst from the stone and gushed out in a stream, enough for everyone.

Exodus chapters 15 to 17

The Ten Commandments

After three months of wandering through the hot, rocky desert, the Israelites arrived at the foot of the holy mountain of Sinai. Moses announced they would camp there a while. He told them that they should make ready with prayers and rituals because in three days' time God was going to speak to all of them.

Sure enough, on the morning of the third day, black storm clouds gathered around the peak of the mountain, hiding it from view. Thunder rumbled and lightning split the skies. Then the earth shook, and the mountain began to spew out flames and smoke as if it were an enormous furnace. A sound like a giant trumpet blared out through the air, calling the terrified Israelites to assemble at the foot of the mountain. Then Moses slowly climbed up and up towards the smoking, fiery mountain-top and disappeared from view into the clouds.

For a long time after he had gone, thunder continued to echo around the slopes and many Israelites thought it was the voice of God talking to their leader. When the noise had at last died away, Moses came back down the mountain and announced that God had given him ten important rules of behaviour:

1. *You should not worship any other god but me.*

2. *You should not make a statue or a picture to worship.*

3. *You should only use my name respectfully.*

4. *You should keep the seventh day, or Sabbath, of every week as a holy day of rest.*

5. *You should always be respectful to your parents.*

6. *You should never commit murder.*

7. *You should never be unfaithful to your partner.*

8. *You should not steal.*

9. *You should not lie.*

10. *You should not envy the things that other people have.*

Moses wrote the Ten Commandments down, and lots of lesser rules too. The very next day he built an altar at the foot of the mountain and asked the Israelites to vow to obey the rules. Then Moses made a sacrifice to seal their solemn promise.

Yet God still had more that He wanted the Israelites to learn, so He summoned Moses up the mountain once more, where they could talk on their own together. The Israelites watched as their leader climbed up the mountain one more time and disappeared alone into the dark clouds.

The Israelites watched and waited for Moses to return… watched and waited for seven long weeks, but there was no sign of their leader. Worried and confused, they came to the conclusion that God had abandoned them and Moses would never return.

"Make something for us to worship," they begged Aaron. "We need something we can see and touch." Thousands of men and women brought Aaron their gold jewellery. He melted it down and made an enormous statue of a calf, one of the animals that was sometimes sacrificed to God. To please the people and keep them under control, Aaron even built the calf an enormous altar and declared there would be a festival in its honour.

The people were delighted. At last they had a straightforward god. One that wasn't invisible and didn't speak to them in thunder, giving them complicated lists of things they should and shouldn't do. Immediately, the Israelites began praying to the calf and offering it sacrifices, and singing and dancing around it.

As they did so, Moses came clambering down the mountainside at last. He held two huge stone tablets on which God Himself had written out the ten most important commandments so that no one could forget them or get them wrong.

Moses knew already about how the Israelites were worshipping the golden calf because God had told him while they were

up the mountain. God had been full of fury
and so was Moses. Enraged at the sight that
met his eyes as he approached the camp,
he flung the stone tablets to the ground
and they shattered into pieces. Then
he hurled the golden calf into the
flames of one of the sacrificial fires.
"Aaron, what did everyone do to
you that you allowed this to
happen?" Moses spat
with disgust at
his brother. Then
he called for
anyone who was
on God's side to go
and stand next to him. Only the
men of the tribe of Levi took up places next

to Moses. On God's orders, he told each of them to grab a sword and put to death everyone who stood in their way as punishment for their sins.

Over three thousand Israelites were killed that night. The next day, Moses went back up the mountain to pray to God for forgiveness for the wickedness of His Chosen People.

Exodus chapters 19 to 24, 32

The Ark and the Tabernacle

Moses returned from Mount Sinai having renewed the Israelites' vow to serve God. He carried two new stone tablets on which God had again written the Ten Commandments. This time, Moses' face glowed from having talked with God. The light was so bright that people couldn't look

straight at him, so from then on Moses wore
a veil.

Moses told the people that God wanted
them to build an ornate chest to keep
copies of all His laws in. They also had to
make a special tent in which they could
worship God until they reached a place
where they could build a proper temple.
God told Moses that the chest was to be
called the Ark of the Covenant and the tent
was to be known as the Tabernacle.

After everything that had happened, the
Israelites were only too glad to be forgiven
and given another chance. They gave their
gold, silver, jewels, rare woods and fine
cloths to the project and set to work.

They built the tent with an outer wall of

bronze pillars and curtains that hung from silver rods. The curtain at the eastern end was richly sewn in violet, purple and scarlet, and formed the entrance. At the opposite end was the Tabernacle itself. The Israelites made this from wooden boards covered with gold and set on silver pillars, supporting four layers of curtains. The Tabernacle was divided into two rooms. One was for men to pray in, and the other room was called the Holy of Holies and was where the Ark of the Covenant was kept. Only the High Priest was allowed to enter this room on one special day of the year. The Israelites made the chest out of wood, covered with gold, with two carved angels covering the top with their wings.

God sent a cloud of glory to cover the Tabernacle. Whenever the cloud lifted, the Israelites knew it was time to pack up camp and continue their journey in the wilderness. Wherever the cloud settled, they knew they should rest. To move the Ark, the Israelites slotted rods through holes in its sides. They used the rods to carry the Ark because they believed that anyone who touched it would die. Wherever the Israelites went, they carried the Ark of the Covenant at the head of their procession as a sign that God was always with them.

Exodus chapters 34 to 40; Numbers chapter 9

Balaam's Donkey

After many more years wandering in the wilderness, at last God thought the Israelites had earned the right to enter Canaan, the land he had long ago promised Abraham would be theirs.

The Israelites would have to fight for it, as many warlike tribes lived there. However, years of travelling through the desert had made the Israelites tough. They had become a ruthless people of fearless fighters, with a firm belief that God was on their side. They approached Canaan, conquering the villages, towns and cities one by one.

There came a time when the Israelites were surrounding the lands of Balak, King of Moab. King Balak was afraid and sent messengers to his fortune-teller, Balaam, to ask him to put a curse on the Israelites.

To the messengers' astonishment, Balaam refused to do so. "The God of the Israelites has spoken to me," he explained. "I must not curse them because they are His Chosen People. Even if the king gave me his palace filled with treasure, I still would not do it."

"Then you will have to come with us," the messengers ordered, and the next morning they dragged him off on a donkey to explain himself to the king.

The donkey wouldn't do a thing it was told. The men were travelling down the road when suddenly the donkey shied away and ran into a field. The animal had been shocked by an angel of God suddenly appearing and barring the way with a drawn sword! Balaam hadn't seen anything and punished the donkey by hitting her. Then the angel appeared on a path between two walls.

The donkey was frightened and pressed against one of the walls, crushing Balaam's foot, so he beat her again. Then, as they were travelling on a narrow path, the angel appeared once more. This time there was no room to turn around. The donkey could only lie down, and Balaam beat her again with a stick.

All at once the donkey yelled, "What are you hitting me for?" God had granted her the power of speech, and He suddenly allowed Balaam to see the angel too.

The man fell to the ground, begging for forgiveness. When he finally reached the king, instead of putting a curse on the Israelites, he blessed them.

Numbers chapters 22 to 24

Joshua and the Battle of Jericho

The Israelites had to fight against the tribes in the lands around Canaan for many years. So many that Moses never got to enter the country that God had chosen for his people. When the time drew near that Moses realized he was going to die, he climbed up to a mountain-top and

God showed him the Promised Land spread out far below. And so Moses died comforted, and a warrior called Joshua took over as ruler of the Israelites.

Then God told Joshua to be brave and bold. It was finally time to cross the River Jordan, which was all that remained to keep the Israelites from entering the Promised Land. So Joshua told the people to prepare to fight. Meanwhile, he sent spies across the river into the city of Jericho to find out what they were up against. The spies were nearly discovered by soldiers because the king of Jericho had heard that enemies had entered the city. He sent troops to search for them, but a woman called Rahab helped the spies escape. In return, she asked for their promise that Joshua's army would not harm her family when they invaded, and the spies agreed. Joshua learnt about the city and the strength of the mighty walls that surrounded it. He drew up battle plans and prayed to God for help.

Then came the day when Joshua gathered the Israelites on the banks of the River Jordan and commanded everyone to listen carefully. "As soon as the priests carrying the Ark of the Covenant at the front step into the river, the waters will stop flowing," Joshua announced. "As long as they stand holding the Ark in the river, there will be dry land and we will all be able to cross safely to the other side."

To the Israelites' astonishment and joy, it happened exactly as their leader had said. Finally, Joshua's army of forty thousand men stood on a plain in the Promised Land.

The walls of the mighty city of Jericho were thick and high, and the city gates were barred against them. But Joshua listened to God, who told him exactly what to do.

Every day for six days, the Israelite army marched around the city walls. Behind the soldiers, priests equipped with trumpets made of rams' horns carried the Ark of the Covenant.

For Jericho's people it was a terrifying and mysterious display of strength. What

are the Israelites up to they wondered?
Does that Ark really have magical powers?
And why are they marching in that eerie
silence? When will they attack?

Then on the seventh day the silence
ceased and an almighty noise began.
Joshua gave the order for the priests to
blow their horns for all they were worth as
the army marched six times around the
city walls. As they began a seventh circuit,
Joshua signalled for his soldiers to shout
as loud as they could. Then
such a roaring joined the
blaring of the horns that
the walls of Jericho
trembled… and then
shook… and then with

a fearful rumble, collapsed to the ground.

Joshua's army entered the city and killed every man, woman and child they found there – all except for Rahab and her household, as she had been promised.

Deuteronomy chapter 34; Joshua chapters 1 to 6

Gideon the Hero

Joshua, the great Israelite army commander, spent his life leading battles against the peoples of the Promised Land of Canaan. He conquered the country and shared it out among the twelve tribes of Israel. But the leaders who followed in his place weren't as strong. Many Israelites

forgot all about God and the great things
He had done for them, and began to
worship idols instead. God, of course, was
furious. As punishment, He sometimes left
the ungrateful Israelites to be attacked and
defeated by enemies.

About two hundred years after Joshua's
death, a desert people called the Midianites
began attacking the Israelites. They
ambushed without warning, slaughtering
the Israelites, trampling their fields and
destroying their crops. As they left they took
all the sheep, cattle and donkeys with them.
Many Israelites took to hiding in the hills,
and a young man called Gideon was
among them.

Gideon was threshing wheat one day

when suddenly he noticed a stranger sitting under a nearby oak tree. Gideon was startled because he hadn't noticed the stranger arrive.

"You are a brave and mighty man," the stranger said. "God is with you."

"Do you mean me?" Gideon queried, looking around him. "And if God is with us Israelites – the God who did such wonderful things years ago, leading our ancestors out of slavery in Egypt – then how come He has abandoned us to the Midianites?"

"No, I mean you," said the stranger. "God wants you to defeat the Midianites."

"Me?" Gideon laughed. "I couldn't lead a rebellion! My tribe of Manasseh is the least important of the twelve tribes of Israel, my family is the least important in the tribe and I am the least important in my family."

"God will help you and you will crush the Midianites," insisted the stranger.

"Prove it then," said Gideon, laughing. "But first, stay and eat with me."

"Very well," said the stranger, and Gideon went to fetch some bread, meat and broth. He set them on a flat rock, then the stranger touched them with his walking staff. There was a blinding flash and everything, including the stranger, disappeared.

Then Gideon was terrified, he knew he had been face to face with an angel. He heard God speak in his mind, saying, "Don't be afraid, Gideon, all will be well."

Soon, news came that the Midianites were preparing for another raid. "Now!" God told Gideon, and sent him signs to prove that the time had come. So Gideon sent messengers to call the four nearest Israelite tribes to him to prepare to fight.

To his astonishment, Gideon soon found he had an army of thirty-two thousand men. "Too many," God told him. "If this many people fight, they will say they won by their own strength, not by my help. Tell everyone who is afraid to go home." Gideon did so, and only ten thousand

remained. "Still too many," sighed God.
"Take everyone down to the river to drink.
Those who lap up the water with their
tongues can stay, those who scoop up water
in their hands must go." After this, Gideon
had only three hundred people left. "That's
better," God said, and explained
what he should do next.

That night, Gideon gave each
man a trumpet and a torch covered
by a jar, so its light was dim. He split
the fighters into three groups and sent
them creeping up on the Midianite
camp from different directions. When
Gideon signalled, the men blew their
trumpets for all they were worth,
shouting, "For God and for Gideon!"

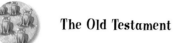

and they smashed the jars so the torches blazed in the darkness.

Of course, the Midianites woke up confused and terrified, thinking that a mighty army was attacking them. In the darkness and the panic, many began fighting each other. The rest ran for their lives, and were chased and killed by Gideon and his men.

And the Israelites were able to live in peace for forty years, until the brave and mighty Gideon died.

Judges chapters 2, 6 to 8

Samson the Strong

The Israelites suffered for many years at the hands of a people called the Philistines. However one day an angel appeared to an Israelite couple and gave a prediction: "You will have a son who will fight for Israel against the Philistines. You must raise him to worship God according to

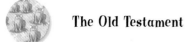
the strict rules of the Nazirite sect, and one of these rules is that you must be careful never to cut his hair."

The couple were overjoyed when they did indeed have a baby boy. They called their little son Samson, but he didn't stay little for long. God ensured that Samson grew up to be tall and strong. He was so strong that once, when he was attacked by a lion, he killed it with his bare hands!

To his parents' immense dismay, Samson fell in love with a Philistine girl, and he insisted on marrying her. At the wedding, Samson set his bride's guests a difficult riddle. They tried for three days to work it out but couldn't come up with the answer. In the end, they pestered the bride to find out, and she persuaded Samson to tell her so she could tell them. Samson realized what his new wife had done. In a temper, he killed thirty Philistines, and stormed off back home. By the time he calmed down and returned to reclaim his bride, she had married someone else! Samson was so furious that he burned the Philistine harvest fields. When the Philistines found out why, they burned down the house of his

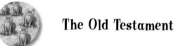

former bride in turn. With this, Samson's rage knew no bounds and he single-handedly killed many more Philistines before he returned home.

From then on Samson was the Philistines' enemy. They demanded that some Israelites from the tribe of Judah hand him over, or face the consequences. The men explained the situation to Samson, and Samson agreed to be bound and taken to his enemies. But once surrounded, he burst out of his ropes and attacked the Philistines, grabbing a nearby bone to use as a weapon. He left them all for dead before escaping.

Eventually the giant man became the leader of all Israel. He ruled for twenty years, but the Philistines never gave up trying to capture him. Once, they waited until Samson was in the city of Gaza. They knew he would leave the next morning and planned to attack him by surprise at the city gates. But when they went there at dawn, they found that Samson had outsmarted them. He had left in the middle of the night, uprooting the massive, locked gates and carrying them off!

The Philistines saw yet another chance to take revenge on Samson when he fell in love with a woman called Delilah. Philistine chiefs visited Delilah and promised to pay her five thousand and five hundred pieces of silver if she handed him over to them. So each time Samson visited Delilah, she tested his great strength and tried to persuade him to tell her the secret of it. Eventually, Samson gave in. "My parents promised God that I would never have my hair cut," he explained. "If I cut my hair, I lose God's protection and my strength will be gone."

Delilah's eyes lit up. At last, she knew! Next time Samson came to visit, she gave him wine and gradually he fell asleep.

Then she cut off his hair and called the Philistines. It wasn't enough for Samson's enemies to bind him in chains, they blinded him too. Then they threw him in prison and set him to work as a slave.

Around a year passed, and the day came when the Philistines held a great festival in honour of their god, Dagon. The temple was so crowded that three thousand people spilled out onto the roof. There were prayers, songs, dances, poems and plays. Everyone enjoyed themselves immensely. Then people began shouting for Samson to be brought in, so they could mock the former great Israelite chief.

As the huge, blind man was led into the centre of the temple amid jeers, shouts and insults, no one thought anything of the fact that his hair had grown back. And as the crowd booed, hissed and cursed him, no one heard Samson pray, "Oh God, give me back my strength just one last time." Samson stretched out his hands to his right and left and God helped him find the cold marble of the two main pillars of the temple. Then Samson gave a mighty roar. He pushed and heaved and strained. Amid screams and howls of terror, the huge pillars toppled apart and the temple crashed to the ground in ruins.

And so Samson died, taking many thousands of his enemies with him.

Judges chapters 13 to 16

Ruth the Loyal

Once, there was a terrible famine around Bethlehem. A starving man called Elimelech journeyed with his wife, Naomi, and two sons to live in Moab, where things were better. Then quite suddenly Elimelech died. Naomi and her sons were grief-stricken, but they tried to carry on as Elimelech would have wanted. The boys married, Moabite girls called Ruth and Orpah. But then tragedy struck again – both boys died. Naomi was heartbroken.

"I am going to return home," Naomi told Ruth and Orpah, but Ruth refused to see the old, lonely widow go off on her own. "Where you go, I go," Ruth vowed. "Your people will be my people, your god, my god."

Naomi smiled gratefully through her tears, and she and Ruth journeyed back to Bethlehem together.

Ruth and Naomi were now very poor. They struggled to make a living. One day, Ruth was in the fields at harvest time, collecting up the leftover corn when she caught the eye of the farm-owner, a man called Boaz. He stopped and asked who she was. Boaz happened to be a cousin of Naomi's and he did what he could to help Ruth. Boaz told her she was welcome in his fields all the time. He told his harvesters to let her drink from their water jars whenever she wanted. He even invited Ruth to join his harvesters for a meal, giving her enough food to take home for supper. Boaz also secretly told his harvesters to leave extra corn behind so Ruth would have more to pick up.

Day after day, Boaz showed Ruth small kindnesses like these, and eventually Naomi dared to send Ruth to ask Boaz formally for his protection.

Boaz was delighted. As was tradition, he went to the city gate and declared in public that he wanted to look after Ruth and Naomi. Boaz and Ruth were married, and Boaz cared for the women all their lives.

So Ruth was rewarded for her loyalty and kindness to Naomi, and Naomi was comforted in her old age. In the fullness of time, God sent Ruth a baby boy, Obed, who brought the two women happiness. They never dreamt that Obed would have a son called Jesse, who would have a son called David, who would one day become the greatest king Israel ever had.

Ruth chapters 1 to 4

Samuel the Servant

Samuel was a little boy who lived with Eli, the high priest at the temple in Shiloh, where the Ark of the Covenant was kept. Samuel's mother Hannah had promised God that her son would serve Him all his life and learn how to be a priest one day.

Eli was a good man who looked after Samuel lovingly. He had two sons of his own, but they grew up to be wicked and violent while Samuel was good and obedient.

One night, the little boy was woken by Eli calling his name. "Here I am!" Samuel called, and hurried to see what the high priest wanted.

"It wasn't me who called you," said Eli, quite confused. "Go back to bed, son."

But a while later, Samuel was again woken by Eli calling his name. "Here I am!" he cried again, and dashed off to find Eli.

"It wasn't me who called you!" Eli reassured Samuel. "Now go back to bed, like a good boy."

But an hour or so later, the voice came again. "Samuel! Samuel!" And Samuel rushed off once more to Eli.

"Samuel," the old high priest said quietly, "I think it must be God who is calling you, and I think you're going to hear Him again. The next time it happens, don't come and find me. Instead call out, 'Speak, Lord, your servant is listening'."

Samuel went back and laid down on his bed in the darkness. And sure enough, the voice came again, "Samuel! Samuel!"

"Speak, Lord, your servant is listening," Samuel replied, just as Eli had told him.

God spoke to Samuel and gave him a difficult message to give the old high priest. A day would come when God was going to punish Israel for its sins and Eli would be punished too, for his sons' wickedness.

In the morning, Samuel was afraid to tell Eli what God had said. When he finally did, the high priest wasn't angry with him. Instead, he hung his head in shame and sadness. "Let God do what He thinks is right," the old man said humbly.

That was the first of many messages that God gave Samuel. For Samuel grew up to be a great prophet who became the ruler of Israel, and was known throughout the land for always speaking the truth.

I Samuel chapters 1 to 3

David and the Giant

The people of Israel saw that other nations had kings to rule them and demanded that they should have one too. The great prophet Samuel asked God for approval. He was told to choose a man called Saul from the tribe of Benjamin to be the first king of Israel.

King Saul won many victories against Israel's enemies, but he did not always do as God wanted. For this reason, God told Samuel that Saul's sons would never be king. God ordered that Samuel travel to Bethlehem and find a shepherd boy called David, the youngest son of a man called Jesse. It was David that God wanted to be the next king. Samuel did so, and gave David a special blessing, and from then on God was always with him.

King Saul's army often had to fight the Philistines because they were constantly invading Israelite territory. Every Israelite who could be spared was called to defend their lands, and three of Jesse's other sons went to the frontline. One day, Jesse sent

David off with food supplies for them. He reached the camp as a battle was beginning and the armoured soldiers were marching onto the battlefield. Suddenly, they all turned and came running back in fear.

"Whatever is going on?" David called as one terrified soldier ran past.

The man just shouted, "Look!" and pointed behind him.

Striding out in front of the Philistine army was a warrior more enormous than David could have dreamt. He was almost twice as big as everyone else!

"Run away if you like," the giant bellowed.

"There's no need to do battle if you're too cowardly. Just send someone to fight me in single combat. Whoever wins has victory for their side. Now, is any one of you men big enough to take up the challenge?" He smashed his mighty spear against his shield and threw back his head and roared, and the noise crashed around the surrounding hills like thunder.

David was outraged. "How dare he! It's an insult not just to us but to God!" he spat. "Just let me at him! Out in the pastures, I've killed lions and bears when they've attacked my father's flocks and I can do the same to this beast too! God protected me then as He will protect me now."

"Well..." said Saul, casting around for

other volunteers. None were forthcoming.
"Very well, and God be with you." Saul
insisted on dressing David in his own
armour, but it was so big and bulky that he
couldn't move, so David took it off again.
He strode out to meet the giant, Goliath of
Gath, with just his staff, his slingshot and
five smooth stones in his shepherd's pouch.

King Saul and his army watched in
amazement. The giant was roaring with
laughter as a mere child walked towards
him. The young boy was yelling back that
he was going to slay Goliath in the name of
God. The shepherd boy stood firm as the
giant ran towards him with death in his
eyes, brandishing his spear. Then David
raised his slingshot and whirled it around

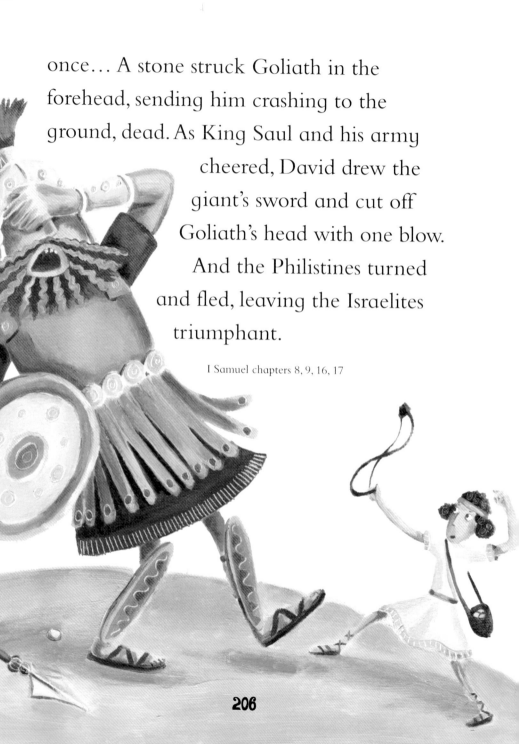

once… A stone struck Goliath in the forehead, sending him crashing to the ground, dead. As King Saul and his army cheered, David drew the giant's sword and cut off Goliath's head with one blow. And the Philistines turned and fled, leaving the Israelites triumphant.

I Samuel chapters 8, 9, 16, 17

Solomon the Wise

When Saul, the first king of Israel died, David came to the throne, just as God had wanted. It was King David who made Israel a great, unified nation with Jerusalem as its capital city. He had the Ark of the Covenant brought there amid great rejoicing. He wanted to build a glorious

temple to house it, but God told David that
He was going to entrust that job to his son,
Solomon, the third king of Israel.

Solomon was in his early twenties when
he took over the throne. He was determined
to carry on his father's good work,
strengthening the nation and keeping peace
with Israel's enemies, but he wasn't sure
exactly how to do it. He felt he lacked the
experience and confidence he needed to be
a good king.

One night, God appeared to Solomon in
a dream and asked how He could help.
"Please, God, give me the gift of wisdom,"
the king begged.

God was delighted. Solomon could have
asked God to give him gold or long life or

power over his enemies, or a whole range of other selfish things. Wisdom to govern the people well was an excellent choice and God was only too happy to oblige.

Not long afterwards, two women who were in the middle of a bitter argument were brought before Solomon so he could settle their dispute. The women lived together and both had recently given birth to a child. However, one of the babies had died, and now each woman was claiming the living baby as hers.

"It's her baby who died," the first one insisted to Solomon. "Do you think I don't know my own child?"

"No, her baby died!" the second woman protested. "Then she stole mine."

Solomon signalled for the women to be quiet. After a few minutes he announced, "Bring me my sword!" As the weapon was fetched he continued, "Cut the child in two and give half to each woman!"

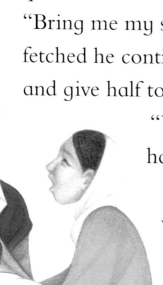

"Yes, neither of us should have him!" cried one woman. But the other burst out wailing. "Sire, please! I would rather see him given away to her than for him to be hurt!"

Then Solomon knew who the real mother of the baby was. And all the people of Israel knew that such wisdom could only have come from God.

II Samuel chapters 5 to 7; I Kings chapters 1, 3

Solomon the Magnificent

The nation of Israel prospered under King Solomon. He kept peace in his lands and trading routes thrived as merchants could travel in safety. He ruled wisely and well, stunning everyone with his incredible knowledge. Then Solomon began to fulfil his father's dream of building a

glorious temple, just as God had said he
would. After nearly five hundred years, the
Ark of the Covenant was to have a home.

Solomon drafted thousands of workers to
build the temple. It was made from
beautiful cedar wood, which came from the
lands of a friend of his, King Hiram of Tyre
in Lebanon. Solomon wanted to use only
the finest materials and the
newest, most exciting
techniques, even if it meant
going to great lengths and
expense to bring materials and
craftspeople from abroad.
Labourers spent years building
massive stone pillars, carving enormous
doors and wooden wall panels with angels

and intricate flowers, dying and weaving beautiful curtains, and lining whole rooms with gold, which were then decorated with stunning jewels.

The day finally came when Solomon ordered the temple to be filled with treasures and the Ark of the Covenant brought to its new home. It was done with such procession and celebrating that no one had ever seen anything like it. As the priests were leaving the temple, the building was suddenly filled with a blazing light so bright that no one could look at it. The king stood in front of the altar before all of his people and gave thanks to God, praying that He would always be with the nation of Israel. Then began a week of feasting.

Solomon didn't stop his building plans at the temple. He erected a magnificent palace and splendid buildings in Jerusalem and Canaan. Rulers from far-off countries travelled to see the marvels for themselves. Even the Queen of Sheba made a journey of fifteen hundred miles through the desert in a camel train laden down with spices, jewels and gold. The queen was amazed – not just by Solomon's incredible buildings but by the wisdom with which he ran the country. "Praise be to your God," she exclaimed, "for He must be hugely pleased with what you have done in His honour."

I Kings chapters 4 to 8, 10

Elijah, Man of God

In the days of King Solomon, one way that eastern kings showed their greatness was to have lots of wives. Solomon had one thousand! Most came from abroad, the marriages arranged to seal peace or trade agreements with other rulers. When Solomon married these foreign women, he let them keep the customs of their country, including worshipping strange idols. Many of the wives talked Solomon into worshipping them too. God was so furious at this that He punished Solomon by splitting up the nation of Israel.

When Solomon died, only two of the twelve tribes of Israel asked his son to be their king, and his nation came to be known as Judah. The other ten tribes wanted one of Solomon's advisors to rule them instead – they kept the name of Israel for their nation. Both kings turned out to be bad. They, and many of the kings who came after, forgot to be faithful to God at all. God had to seek out good people to speak for Him, to remind everyone what

was right and wrong. The people He chose
were called prophets, and one very
important one was a man called Elijah.

Elijah lived in Israel when a wicked king
called Ahab was on the throne, with his
even more wicked queen, Jezebel. They both
worshipped the idol Baal and of course the
people followed them. God sent Elijah to
tell the king how he was going to be
punished. "God says there will be no rain or
dew in your kingdom for three years,"
Elijah announced, then he fled from Ahab's
fury and hid for the duration of the
drought. God worked miracles to keep
Elijah alive as the food ran out and water
dried up all over Israel. He even gave Elijah
the power to work miracles of his own, such

as bringing a dead child back to life.

After three years, God told Elijah to meet King Ahab on the top of Mount Carmel. Elijah told the king to bring the four hundred and fifty prophets of Baal and the four hundred prophets of the false goddess Asherah. "Now let's see who is real and who isn't – Baal and Asherah, or God," Elijah challenged. "Tell your prophets to build an altar and offer a bull as sacrifice to Baal. I'll do the same. Then let us pray for flames to light the sacrificial fire and see who is answered."

And so the king's prophets built an enormous altar and killed a bull. Then they began dancing and singing around it, calling for Baal to light the fire. All afternoon they went on, but nothing happened.

"You might have to sing louder and dance harder than that," Elijah laughed. "Perhaps Baal is busy with other things, or maybe he's gone on a trip, or perhaps he's asleep?"

Then Elijah got on with building a little altar to God for his bull. He used a bundle of firewood and twelve stones (to represent the tribes of God's Chosen People). He drenched everything with water until it was completely soaked and filled a trench he had dug around it. Then he stood and said a quiet prayer – a still, lone figure compared to the hundreds of excited, chanting prophets of Baal.

Instantly, fire blazed from Heaven and burned up not just Elijah's bull, but also the wood, the stones, the earth around about – everything. Even the trench full of water hissed and sizzled, and vanished into steam.

The watching crowds fell to the ground in terror.

Then Elijah told Ahab that all the prophets of Baal and Asherah should be put to death, and no one should ever worship idols again. "By the way," Elijah added casually, "you should get a move on if you don't want to get drenched on your way home." For the skies suddenly darkened

with black thunder clouds as God prepared
to send Israel rain at last.

God stayed with Elijah for the rest of his
life and looked after him. Over the years
He spoke many prophecies through him
that all came true. God also told Elijah to
travel to Syria and find a man called Elisha,
whom God wanted as another important
prophet. Elijah did so, and Elisha became
his constant companion. Elisha was so loyal
that he never left his master Elijah's side,
even when the time came that the old man
knew he was to die. At that moment, a
chariot of fire drawn by blazing horses
came thundering towards the two men,
forcing them apart. Elisha saw Elijah swept
up into the chariot and off into the sky as if

by a mighty whirlwind. It circled higher
and higher until it became a tiny speck and
finally disappeared from view.

And so Elijah was gone, leaving behind
only his cloak, lying on the ground.
Elisha picked it up and walked down to
the nearby River Jordan. He lashed the
river with the cloak and cried out,
"Where is the God
of Elijah?"

To his astonishment, the
waters drew back and
parted before him.
Then Elisha
knew that God
was with him as
He had been with
Elijah, and it was
up to him to
carry on where
Elijah had left off.

I Kings chapters 11, 12, 14 to 19;
II Kings chapter 2

223

Elisha and the Leper General

Elisha the holy man travelled around Israel, speaking prophecies for God and working miracles. God gave him so much power that Elisha even once brought a dead child back to life, just as his former master, the prophet Elijah, had done.

News of Elisha's miracles spread far and

wide and all sorts of people, rich and poor, begged him for help. One of them was the commander-in-chief of the Syrian army, General Naaman. He suffered from the terrible skin disease, leprosy. He arrived in his smartest uniform, in a huge convoy of gleaming chariots and bodyguards to see Israel's great miracle worker.

This sort of thing didn't impress Elisha. He didn't even bother to come to the door to see the general. He just sent a servant outside with a message: "Wash in the River Jordan seven times and you will be cured."

Well, General Naaman wasn't used to being treated like that. He huffed about in a terrible temper, shouting things like: "The River Jordan is nothing compared to the mighty rivers we have back home in Syria! Why should I wash in a little puddle like that?" It took all Naaman's men to calm him down and convince him to try it.

Six times General Naaman washed himself in the rushing River Jordan. When he emerged after the seventh, his skin was healed.

The overjoyed general hurried back to Elisha and begged him to accept a fortune in silver and gold as a thank you.

All the prophet would have was Naaman's promise to worship God from then on.

However, Elisha's servant Gehazi was tempted by the sight of the treasure. When the general set off back to Syria, he galloped after him and lied that Elisha had changed his mind and he would like some money after all. Naaman delightedly sent Gehazi back with as much treasure as a couple of his own servants could carry.

Of course, Elisha mysteriously knew what Gehazi had done. "You have enough money now to buy splendid possessions," he announced to his servant, "but you have also bought Naaman's leprosy too."

In horror, Gehazi looked down to see his hands fester with sores. He stumbled out of Elisha's house with the skin all over his body turning white and dead. Gehazi had been made a leper.

II Kings chapters 4, 5

Jonah and the Giant Fish

O ne day, God told a man called Jonah, "Go to Assyria, to the capital city of Nineveh. Tell the wicked people there about me and make sure they change their sinful ways."

Now Jonah didn't care for these people and wasn't much bothered if they found out

about God or not. He also didn't like the
sound of walking into the capital city of a
powerful, war-like nation and telling the
people what they were doing wrong. So
Jonah got on a boat in the opposite
direction to Nineveh, heading for Spain.

As soon as the ship was on its way, God
sent a mighty storm its way. The sailors
were terrified and began praying to be
saved. Still the rain lashed the boat and the
wind and waves hurled it this way and that.
Then the sailors decided that someone on
board must be cursed. They drew lots and
came up with Jonah's name. Shamefully,
Jonah confessed that he was disobeying
God by being on the boat. "You'll have to
throw me overboard," he wept, "it's the only

way you'll get this storm to stop." The sailors were horrified and did their best to row to shore. But when the storm grew even worse they concluded there was only one thing for it – and dropped Jonah into the water.

The minute they did so, the wind dropped, the rain stopped, the waves died away, and the ship was saved. God saved Jonah too. Instead of letting him sink and drown, He sent a massive fish that

swallowed him. For three
days Jonah wallowed in the stinky
darkness of the fish's belly, praying to
God for another chance. Finally, to
his relief, the fish spat him out
onto a sandy shore.

"Go to Nineveh," God said
again, "and give the people
my message. If they don't
change their behaviour, I will
destroy the city after forty days."
This time Jonah did what he was
told. To his immense surprise the
Assyrians listened. The king of Nineveh
believed God's threat and ordered his people
to mend their ways. Soon, there was a drop
in crime. People started being more polite

and kind to each other. They prayed for forgiveness and fasted, and started worshipping God. The forty days came and went and God left the city and its people untouched.

Jonah stomped off on his own into the countryside. "I knew this would happen!" he moaned to God, sitting down in protest. "I've come all this way – nearly drowned, been eaten by a fish, then walked for miles to face crowds of hostile strangers – and all for nothing. You haven't punished anyone or destroyed anything at all."

God decided to teach the angry man a lesson. He made a tree shoot up swiftly right where Jonah was sitting, so all day he could rest in its cool shade. However the next day, God sent insects to eat the tree so it shrivelled and died, leaving Jonah sitting in the blazing sun. God also sent desert wind to roast him. "If only my poor tree hadn't died!" Jonah groaned.

"Well," said God kindly, "if you're upset about a tree – a tree that you neither planted nor looked after – how upset do you think I would have been if the city of Nineveh had been lost? One hundred and twenty thousand people live there, not to mention all the animals."

And Jonah finally understood that God cared for all people, not just the Israelites – and for animals too. After all, hadn't God made them all in the first place?

Jonah

Jeremiah and the End of the Nation

Centuries passed and numerous kings came and went on the thrones of Israel and Judah, who had to fight many enemies. There came a time when the mighty Assyrians rose up against them. The two nations kept the Assyrian empire at bay by paying an enormous amount of treasure each year. However, the emperor eventually sent his armies to attack Israel. God did not stop them because the Israelites had become too sinful to deserve His help. So the Assyrians crushed the ten tribes of God's Chosen People and took them away in their thousands back to Assyria to be slaves. They filled Israel's capital city of Samaria with captives brought from other lands they had conquered. These settlers became known as Samaritans.

Around one hundred years went by and God chose a young man called Jeremiah to be His prophet in Judah. "You must warn everyone that unless they change their wicked ways, I will send disaster upon them from the north," God told Jeremiah. God meant that Judah would be overcome by another enemy – the Babylonians, who had become even mightier than the Assyrians.

God sent Jeremiah to the house of a potter to watch him shaping clay on his wheel. "Judah is like clay in my hands," God explained to Jeremiah. "If the people do evil, I will crush them. But if they do well, I shall mould them into something good and strong."

Jeremiah told the leaders and people of Judah many times that it was not too late for them to mend their ways. However, they did not listen and God made up his mind that Judah would fall. Jeremiah told the people this and he even took to wearing a yoke, a harness for an ox, around his neck as a sign to everyone that they would soon be made slaves.

The Judeans hated Jeremiah for his prophecies of destruction, but of course they came true. Nebuchadnezzar, king of Babylon, sent a huge army to attack Judah. The city of Jerusalem was taken and most of the people were taken back to Babylon in chains.

"Do not fear," God told Jeremiah, "when my people in exile repent for their sins, I will bring them out of captivity and restore the kingdom of Israel as a united, great nation once more."

II Kings chapters 17, 18, 25; Jeremiah chapters 1, 18, 24, 27, 31, 39

Nebuchadnezzar's Dream

King Nebuchadnezzar, Emperor of Babylon, was very clever. When he conquered other countries and took their peoples captive, he got his officials to look for those who had special talents so he could put them to good use for himself.

Daniel and his three friends Shadrach,

Meshach and Abednego were among a few
young captive Israelite men selected to be
trained as advisors to the king. They worked
hard and God gave them extra skills as a
reward. God made Daniel very good at
telling the meaning of dreams and visions.

One morning, the king called an
emergency meeting of his advisors. "I have
had a worrying dream," Nebuchadnezzar
announced, "and I want someone to
explain to me what it means."

"Tell us the dream, Your Majesty, and
we'll be glad to interpret what it means,"
replied his advisors, bowing low.

"No," announced Nebuchadnezzar, with
a glint in his steely eyes. "You could make
up any meaning you like. I want someone

to tell me both the dream and the meaning. Only then will I be convinced of the truth."

"And by the way," he added coldly, "if no one can do it, I'll have every one of you put to death."

Daniel begged the king for time, and he, Shadrach, Meshach and Abednego asked God for help. And so God sent Daniel a dream, which told him everything.

"You saw a massive statue," Daniel told Nebuchadnezzar. "Its head was gold, its chest and arms silver, its belly and thighs bronze, its legs iron and its feet half iron and half clay. Then an enormous stone bashed against the statue's feet and the statue toppled and smashed into dust. Then the stone grew into a mountain that covered all the earth.

"This dream means that your empire is like the head of gold, greatest of all. The silver, bronze and iron are three kingdoms that will come after yours, each less powerful than the one before. The last kingdom will be divided into two and will be partly strong and partly weak. But no empire will last until God's kingdom comes and replaces all others forever."

Nebuchadnezzar was astonished and delighted. "Your god must indeed be the god of all gods," he marvelled. He rewarded Daniel and made him chief of his wise men.

Daniel chapters 1, 2

Shadrach, Meshach and Abednego

King Nebuchadnezzar gave orders for a gigantic statue to be made, fifteen times larger than a man, and entirely of gold. He commanded it set on a plain near Babylon, and held a grand ceremony to mark its unveiling. A herald announced that whenever a certain piece of music was played, Nebuchadnezzar wanted everyone to bow down in the direction of the statue and worship it.

Daniel's three friends, Shadrach, Meshach and Abednego, were spotted disobeying the king and refusing to bow down to the statue. As faithful Jews, they would only worship the one, true God.

When Nebuchadnezzar heard this he was furious and ordered the three men be bound and flung into the blazing palace furnace. The enraged king even commanded that the furnace be made seven times hotter than usual. It was so hot that it burned the guards who threw Shadrach, Meshach and Abednego in. Nebuchadnezzar was astonished when he looked into the furnace and saw the three men walking about in the blaze. Not only that, but he was sure that he saw a fourth figure – a strange, holy being that he was convinced could only be an angel.

Nebuchadnezzar went as close to the furnace as he dared, and roared, "Come out at once!" Shadrach, Meshach and Abednego stepped out perfectly unharmed.

So Nebuchadnezzar gave orders that no one was to disrespect the God of the Israelites, and he appointed the three men to high and powerful positions of office.

Daniel chapter 3

Belshazzar's Banquet

When Nebuchadnezzar died, Belshazzar became the new king of Babylon. He gave a great feast in his own honour that was to be attended by many of his nobles and his wives.

No expense was spared. Belshazzar even gave orders that the gold and silver cups

plundered from Solomon's temple in
Jerusalem should be used as wine goblets.

The king and his guests laughed and
shouted with enjoyment at the splendid
feast, drinking toasts to their false gods and
idols out of the sacred Israelite cups. Then
quite suddenly, a ghostly hand appeared out
of nowhere and began
writing strange words
slowly upon a white
wall. Belshazzar fell
silent. When the hand
had finished writing
and faded away, he
called for his wise men to
read the words, but no one could do so. The
queen suggested calling Daniel, who was by

now an old man, and so he was sent for.

"It is God who sent the hand you saw," Daniel declared to the king. "The words are *mene, mene, tekel, upharsin.*"

"But can you tell me what they mean?" Belshazzar whispered hoarsely.

"Of course," said Daniel, calmly. "*Mene* means number… The days of your reign are numbered. *Tekel* means weight… You have been weighed to see your worth, and it's not enough. *Upharsin* means division… Your kingdom is going to be divided between the Medes and the Persians."

Daniel's words came true that night. Belshazzar was killed and King Darius of the Medes and Persians seized the throne.

Daniel chapter 5

Daniel in the Lions' Den

Daniel was such an outstanding advisor that King Darius of the Medes and Persians put him in charge of his whole empire. The other officials were so jealous that they came up with an idea that was certain to land Daniel in trouble. They suggested to Darius that he should order that no one should pray to anyone but him for thirty days. If anyone disobeyed, they were to be thrown into a pit of hungry lions. The king thought it was a great idea and signed the order.

Now Daniel was a good, holy man. Of course, he continued to pray to God three times a day, as always in front of his window in full view of passers-by.

It wasn't long before his enemies reported him to the king. Darius was devastated, but he could not go back on his word. He ordered that Daniel should be thrown into the den of lions. "May your god save you," the king prayed, and a huge stone was placed over the pit so there was no way Daniel could escape.

Darius spent all night thinking about how he had caused Daniel to be flung to the lions. As soon as dawn came he hurried to the pit and yelled out, "Daniel! Was God with you? Are you still alive?"

To Darius' relief, Daniel answered, "Yes, sire. God sent an angel to guard me and the lions have left me untouched."

The king ordered that Daniel be pulled out of the pit and all the wicked people who had accused him thrown in instead. The lions tore them to bits until nothing but bones were left.

Daniel chapter 6

Queen Esther
the Brave

King Xerxes was a mighty Persian king whose empire stretched from India to Ethiopia. He was once so displeased with his wife, Vashti, that he announced she was no longer his queen. He ordered for beautiful young women to be brought from all corners of his empire to the palace so he could choose a new wife.

One of the men who worked in the royal household was an old Jew called Mordecai. He urged his adopted daughter Esther to go to the palace and take part in the beauty competition. Mordecai warned her not to tell anyone she was his daughter or that she was Jewish, for many people hated the captives who had been brought from Israel.

Esther did as she was told and went to the palace. For a year she was pampered with beauty treatments, and had lessons in grooming and how to behave like a queen. When all the candidates were presented to the king, Xerxes chose Esther as his queen. He soon found that she wasn't just a pretty face either. He came to like her very much.

One day, she told him how Mordecai had overheard two servants plotting to kill him, and Xerxes believed Esther at once. He had the two men arrested and hanged, and ordered for the event to be written down in his official Book of Records. Mordecai and Esther had saved his life.

Some time later, King Xerxes made a man called Haman his chief minister and commanded his subjects to bow before him. Mordecai always refused. "I bow to none other than God," the old man would insist. This disobedience drove Haman quite mad. He was determined to have revenge. Not just on Mordecai, but on all Jewish people. He told the king that the Jews were disobedient and nothing but trouble, and that his kingdom would be better off if he had them all put to death. "Whatever you think best," Xerxes told his trusted minister, and gave Haman his royal seal to sign the execution warrant.

When Mordecai found out he was appalled, and begged Esther to ask Xerxes for mercy. She dressed in her finest robes and went unsummoned into the king's presence, an action for which the law said she could have been put to death. Luckily, the king was happy to see her and said she could have whatever she had come for.

"All I would like is for you and Haman to be my guests at dinner tomorrow," Esther said charmingly, and the king agreed.

Esther held a wonderful dinner for the

men, with delicious food and witty conversation in beautiful surroundings. Having begun to win her husband and his minister over, she invited them to another dinner the following night, when she hoped she could finish the job and ask for forgiveness for the Jews.

Little did she know that later that very evening Haman had ordered that a gallows be built at the palace. They were to hang the man he hated – Mordecai, her father.

At around the same time, Xerxes was
being read aloud to from the Book of
Records. The reader happened to announce
the entry that described how
Mordecai had helped foil the

earlier plot to kill King Xerxes, and it
reminded the king that he had never
honoured the man.

Just then, a servant announced that
Haman was asking to see him. He had

come to ask for the king's permission to execute Mordecai.

"Now Haman, tell me what you would do to reward a man you wanted to honour," wondered the king, as his chief minister was ushered in.

Haman tried to hide a smug smirk. He thought that he must be the man the king wanted to honour. "Such a person should be dressed in robes fit for a king and paraded on one of your own horses through the streets as a hero," Haman sighed.

"What a good idea!" Xerxes said, delighted. "Then that's what I want you to do for Mordecai the Jew in the morning."

Haman was outraged, yet he had no choice but to do as the king had commanded. By the time he arrived at Esther's second supper, Haman's face was as sulky and ugly as Esther's was beautiful.

This time, the queen begged Xerxes for mercy. She confessed that she was a Jew and that orders had been given for all Jewish people to be put to death.

"Who has dared to do such a terrible thing?" boomed the king, outraged.

"The man who is sitting beside you," Esther said quietly. "Haman."

Xerxes was so choked with fury that he couldn't speak and he strode out into the palace gardens.

He returned to find his chief minister at Esther's feet, grabbing at her skirt. Haman was in fact begging for mercy, but it looked as though he was attacking the king's wife. To make matters worse, one of Esther's servants told the king that Haman had built a gallows to kill Mordecai, the very man who had once helped save Xerxes's life.

The king did not delay in having Haman executed on his own gallows. Then he sent letters throughout his empire, ordering that the Jews should be respected, and allowed to defend themselves if necessary.

And that is how the brave, beautiful Esther saved her people, the Israelites.

Esther chapters 1 to 8

THE NEW TESTAMENT

The New Testament is the name for the second section of the Bible, made up of twenty-seven books. It describes the birth, life and death of a man called Jesus, His teachings about God and His followers. Jesus lived two thousand years ago in the Middle East. At that time, the Romans controlled these lands and the Jewish people who lived there were unhappy about it. They were waiting for a saviour – the 'Messiah' – who would establish a mighty kingdom for them. The New Testament was written by the followers of Jesus, who believed Him to be the Messiah, during the one hundred years after He died.

The Angel Gabriel
Brings News

There once lived in Galilee an old priest called Zachariah and his wife Elizabeth. Both were good Jewish people who always tried to live by God's rules. However, they were sad because they had never been able to have children.

One day Zachariah was given a special

honour. It was his turn to go into the great temple in Jerusalem, to the most sacred altar, and make an offering to God. As he did so, deep in prayer, an angel suddenly appeared. Zachariah was terrified.

"Don't be afraid," the angel said. "I have come with great news. God is going to answer the prayers of you and your wife, begging for children. He is going to give you a son. God wants you to call him John. Your son is going to be a very holy man and will do great work for Him."

Zachariah was stunned. Was he really seeing and hearing an angel? And even if he was, Elizabeth was past the usual age for having children. "Are you sure?" he asked in disbelief. "How can this be?"

"I am Gabriel, a
messenger from God!"
the angel said
sternly. "Because
you haven't
believed me you will stay
silent until it comes true!"
And the angel disappeared, just
as suddenly as he had arrived.

Imagine Elizabeth's surprise when
her husband came home unable to speak.
He had to explain what had happened by
acting things out and writing things down.
Imagine Elizabeth's amazement when a
short while later her husband's prediction
came true and she found that she was
pregnant. Elizabeth was astonished when

six months later, her younger cousin Mary arrived unannounced. All at once Elizabeth knew that Mary was also having a baby – a very special baby indeed.

Just as mysteriously, Mary knew about Elizabeth's baby. Bursting with excitement and happiness, she explained everything to her cousin. Mary had been going about her chores one day as usual when suddenly the angel Gabriel appeared in her little home in the town of Nazareth. It was he who had told her that Elizabeth was going to have a baby. But the angel had even more important news for Mary. Gabriel told her that God thought she was very special and that He was going to make her the mother of His son. Mary was going to have a little boy, and God wanted Mary to call him Jesus. "He will be ruler over all the Lord's people and His Kingdom will have no end," the angel told the stunned woman.

Mary hurried off to visit Elizabeth straight away so she could share her joy with her cousin. She stayed as long as she could to help the older lady through her pregnancy. But before Elizabeth's baby was born, Mary had to return home to prepare for the birth of her own child.

Luke chapter 1

שְׁמוֹ
הוּא
יוֹחָנָן

His Name is John

The day came when Elizabeth gave birth to a baby boy just as the angel Gabriel had said. Her neighbours and relatives came to admire the new arrival. Everyone marvelled at what a miracle it was that Elizabeth had been able to have a baby at her age.

When the baby was one week old, the
family held a party to promise him to God
and to officially name him. Everyone
assumed that the couple were going to call
the boy Zachariah because it was tradition
for the first son to be named after his father.
Elizabeth caused a stir when she announced
that the baby was to be named John.

"John!" Elizabeth's relations exclaimed.
"There's no one in our family called John.
Where on earth have you come up with
that name from?" Turning to Zachariah,
they asked, "Zachariah, you want your son
to be named after you, don't you? Of
course you do! Tell Elizabeth immediately."

Poor Zachariah still couldn't speak. Very
frustrated, he signalled around for

something to write with. Someone hurried
to find him a writing tablet. Then
Zachariah wrote the biggest, boldest letters
he could fit on the tablet
and then held it up so
everyone could see. It read:
HIS NAME IS JOHN

Everyone grumbled,
but in the midst of their
murmurings Zachariah suddenly
found he could speak again. "My voice has
come back!" he cried. "Thank you, God,
for everything you have done for us!"

It wasn't long before the news of what
had happened at the party had spread far
and wide.

Luke chapter 1

The Birth of Jesus

Mary was engaged to marry a young man called Joseph, a local carpenter. When she told Joseph she was expecting a baby he was very upset. The baby couldn't be his because they weren't married. And in those days, if a single woman was expecting a baby it was quite shameful. However,

Joseph had a dream in which an angel told him, "Don't be afraid to take Mary as your wife. Her baby is the Son of God Himself. The prophets of long ago foretold that He would come and save everyone from their sins. Raise Him as your own son. God wants you to call Him Jesus." After this Joseph felt much better. He realized he would be honoured to bring the little boy up as his own, and he and Mary were married straight away.

However, near the time that the baby was to be born, another problem arose. The emperor Augustus Caesar ordered a survey of all the people in his lands. He commanded that every man had to travel to where he was born, taking his family

with him to have their names put on a
register. Joseph had been born in the city of
Bethlehem in Judea, in southern Israel,
which was quite a distance from the village
of Nazareth. Mary was heavily
pregnant and travelling would be
very difficult for her.
Nevertheless, the couple
did not have a choice.
They packed what they
would need for the trip and
set off. Mary couldn't
possibly walk all that
way, so she rode on a
donkey. It was a bumpy and tiring journey
for a woman so close to having a baby.
By the time the couple reached

Bethlehem they were exhausted, hungry and dusty. Joseph began trying to find a room in which they could stay. He trudged with the donkey and Mary from one lodging place to the next. But to the couple's dismay, everywhere was full. The city was bustling with travellers who had come to register for the emperor's survey.

As they were turned away from one place after another, Mary began to feel that the baby was on its way. Hurriedly, Joseph banged on the door of the nearest inn. After a few moments, the busy innkeeper peered outside. "Don't bother asking, we're full," he said, as soon as he saw the travellers.

"Wait, please help us!" cried Joseph, stopping the innkeeper from shutting the door on them. "My wife's about to have a baby. She can't give birth out here in the street! Haven't you got a spare corner somewhere you could squeeze us in?"

"Well…" said the innkeeper, looking at poor Mary in pain on the donkey. "I haven't got a single room to spare, but you're welcome to shelter in my stable if you don't mind the animals."

"Thank you, thank you so much," Joseph said, gratefully shaking the man's hand, and the innkeeper showed them the way to his stable.

It was there, with the donkeys, oxen and sheep looking on, that Mary gave birth to the baby boy who was to be the saviour of the world. She wrapped Him up in cloths

and nestled Him in a manger full of straw.
And baby Jesus was warm and safe, with
His mother and foster father by His side.

Matthew chapter 1; Luke chapter 2

275

The Shepherds' Visit

On the night that Jesus was born, the city of Bethlehem throbbed with people, while the surrounding countryside was peaceful except for a few shepherds and their flocks. The shepherds were taking turns at sleeping and watching. They made sure that the sheep weren't wandering away and kept watch for hungry wolves.

All at once the starry night sky above the shepherds blazed as bright as day. Then it blazed brighter still, too bright for the shepherds to look up. They shielded their eyes from the blinding glare as an angel appeared high overhead. The shepherds were terrified.

"Don't be afraid," came the angel's voice, clear through the still, cold night. "I bring you wonderful news – wonderful news for everyone on Earth. This very night a child has been born who will be the saviour of all people. You can find Him in a stable in Bethlehem, lying in a manger."

The air was filled with singing more beautiful than the shepherds had ever heard, as hundreds of thousands of angels suddenly appeared in the heavens. "Glory to God," they sang. "And peace to all people on Earth."

The shepherds stood transfixed until the angels had finished their song. Then the heavenly music died and the angels faded away.

Could it really be true the shepherds wondered? In ancient stories prophets had predicted for hundreds of years that a man would come who would save everyone from their sins. They called him the Messiah. Maybe he had really come at last. The shepherds hurried off to Bethlehem, to see for themselves. They searched through the streets until they heard the sound of a newborn baby crying from a stable behind an inn. There they found Mary and Joseph looking after baby Jesus. In great excitement, they told the startled couple all that they had seen and heard. Mary fell very quiet, taking it all in.

The shepherds stayed for a while, marvelling at the baby boy who they had been told was the Messiah, but they had to return to their flocks. All the way back they couldn't stop talking about the amazing chorus of angels and how their

words had come true. They told everyone
they met, praising God and giving thanks
for all that they had seen and been told.

Luke chapter 2

A Special Day for Simeon and Anna

When Jesus was one week old, Mary and Joseph held the usual ceremony to promise their son to God and officially name Him. They also made a trip from Bethlehem to Jerusalem. It was traditional for Jewish families to take their first son to the temple there to give thanks to God and

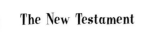

make a sacrifice of two doves or pigeons.

In Jerusalem there lived an old man whose name was Simeon. He was a holy man and had always tried his best to live a good life. God had promised Simeon a reward for his lifetime of faithful service. He promised that he would not die without seeing the Messiah, who was to save the world. For years Simeon longed for this wonderful day to come.

On the morning when Mary and Joseph brought Jesus into the temple, Simeon was already there. God's Holy Spirit had spoken to him earlier, telling him that the day had finally arrived. Simeon hurried to the temple straight away. As soon as the old man caught sight of the tiny baby, he immediately knew who He was.

"Thanks be to God," he cried, taking the little bundle in his arms. "Now I can die in peace because I have seen the saviour who will bring glory to Israel and spread the Word of God to everyone on Earth." Mary and Joseph were amazed.

"Your little child is a sign from God," Simeon continued, "but many people won't believe what He says and will turn against Him." Simeon looked at Mary with great pity in his eyes. "Because of this, great sorrow will one day

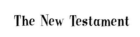

pierce your heart like a sword."

Just then an old woman who visited the temple every day came shuffling over. Her name was Anna and she was a prophetess.

"Can I see my saviour?" she asked. By now, people had begun to crowd around to see what was going on. As Mary and Joseph showed Jesus to Anna, she started telling everyone how the baby came from God and was the hope of the world.

When Mary and Joseph finally left the temple that day, they couldn't help but feel overwhelmed by the amazing events that were happening.

Luke chapter 2

Follow the Star

Far away in distant lands to the east, there lived some wise men who were astrologers. Every night they gazed up at the sky and studied the stars, trying to work out what their movements around the heavens meant for people on Earth. One night they were stunned by a brand new star that appeared much bigger and brighter than the rest. They hurried to consult their ancient books to see what it could mean. The wise men became very excited by what they found, and were in no doubt that a great Jewish prophecy had come true. The star was a sign that a baby had been born who would become the king of God's Chosen People. The wise men decided to set off to find him at once. They packed up their camels with supplies and set off into the desert, heading in the direction of the star that blazed each night in the sky. They arrived in the city of Jerusalem.

News soon reached King Herod of Judea that strangers from the east had arrived in

Jerusalem. These strangers were searching for a newborn baby they were calling the 'King of the Jews'. Of course Herod didn't like the sound of that at all. As far as he was concerned he had been crowned King of the Jews and he wanted it to stay that way. He certainly wasn't going to put up with rumours spreading about a rival – who fulfilled one of the ancient prophecies no less. It would just stir up trouble among the people and they might rise up against him.

King Herod set about dealing with the problem in his cold, calculated way. First, he called a meeting of all the chief Jewish religious leaders to find out more. "Where do your ancient books say the Messiah is to be born?" he asked, innocently.

"In Bethlehem," the holy men answered.

Then King Herod called his guards and ordered them to find the wise men and bring them to him. "But do it in secret," he commanded. "I don't want people to get the impression that I think these men and their rumours are important."

The wise men were nervous when they were summoned to see the king. They had heard that Herod could be a cruel leader. However, they were surprised to find him most polite, interested and even helpful in their quest. "The Jewish elders have told me that you shouldn't be looking in Jerusalem," he explained. "Try Bethlehem instead. When you have found the future king, do come back and tell me all about it.

I'd like to go and pay my respects too."

The wise men had no idea that King Herod only wanted to know where the baby was so he could have him killed.

They set off to Bethlehem and followed the star to where it appeared to hang biggest and brightest in the sky, over the house in

which Mary and Joseph were now staying.
The wise men were surprised to find the
baby in an ordinary home rather than a
splendid palace. They bowed to worship
Him and presented Mary and Joseph with
gifts – jewelled gold caskets, and the rare
spices frankincense and myrrh.

Herod never got to hear of the wise
men's success. The night before they were
due to set off home, they had a troubling
dream that warned them not to return to
the king. The wise men took a different
route back to their lands in the east and
Herod never found them.

Matthew chapter 2

Flight
from Danger

After the wise men had visited Jesus, an angel appeared to Joseph in a dream. "Herod is trying to find the baby to kill Him," the angel warned. "Take Him and Mary to Egypt. It will be a long, hard journey, but it will take you safely out of the cruel king's reach. Stay there until I tell you it is safe to return."

Joseph woke up with a start. He woke Mary and told her to make ready to travel straight away. The family hurried through the dark, sleeping streets of Bethlehem and onto the road to Egypt.

Meanwhile back in Jerusalem, Herod was waiting for the wise men to return from Bethlehem and tell him where the baby king of kings was. He waited… and waited… Eventually he realized that the wise men weren't coming – he had been tricked! Herod flew into a fury and roared at his army chief, "Send your men to search every house in Bethlehem.

I want every boy under two years of age put to death immediately!"

By the time the soldiers arrived in Bethlehem to carry out their terrible task, Jesus, Mary and Joseph were miles away in Egypt. They stayed there for several months until an angel appeared to Joseph once more, telling him that King Herod had died and it was safe to go back to Israel. However Joseph did not take his family back to Bethlehem. The city was far too close to Jerusalem, where King Herod's son was now on the throne. Instead, he travelled north back to their home in the sleepy town of Nazareth in the remote area of Galilee.

Matthew chapter 2

Jesus in the Temple

Every year at the festival of Passover, all Jewish men went visit to the temple in Jerusalem, to pray and give thanks to God. Joseph always went and, like many women, Mary went too. Of course the number of people who crowded into the city was huge. The lodging houses were heaving, people packed streets and the temple itself was totally crammed. Like many parents with young children, Mary and Joseph left Jesus with a relative or neighbour when they went to celebrate the festival. But when He reached the age of twelve, they decided Jesus was old enough to go with them.

The family travelled to Jerusalem with a large group of relatives and friends. When the festival was over, they all set off to travel home. Joseph walked with the men, Mary chatted to the women and Jesus ran back and forth with the other children.

But at the end of the first day's journey, when the group of travellers began to make camp for the night, Jesus had disappeared. Mary and Joseph called for their son at the tops of their voices, but He didn't come. With a rising sense of panic, the couple dashed up and down, describing Jesus to everyone and asking if anyone had seen Him. No one had. Darkness was drawing in fast. "There's nothing else we can do tonight, but as soon as it gets light tomorrow we'll retrace our steps and find Him," Joseph comforted his weeping wife.

Of course, Mary and Joseph didn't sleep for worrying about where Jesus was and whether He was safe. At sunrise Mary and Joseph began making their way back to Jerusalem, asking everyone they met if they had seen a lost twelve-year-old boy. They reached the city and hunted around its bustling streets for two days, but there was no sign of Him.

The third day came and in desperation Mary and Joseph went to look in the great temple itself. To their astonishment, there they found Jesus deep in discussion with a group of Jewish priests and leaders.

"Your son has such a wise understanding of the ancient writings, we can't believe He is only twelve," the holy men told Mary and Joseph. "He asks questions that most people never think to ask, and He's been giving us answers too!"

But Mary and Joseph just wanted to know what had happened to Jesus. "Where on earth have you been?" They cried. "We've been worried sick!"

Jesus replied calmly, "You should have known that you would find me in my Father's house."

Luke chapter 2

John the Baptist

Elizabeth and Zachariah's son John grew up to be a holy man. He went to live on his own in the countryside of Judea, so he could think about God and pray without being distracted. He wore only a simple robe woven from camel hair and survived by eating locusts and wild honey.

When he was about thirty years old, he
began preaching to anyone he came across.
"Be sorry for your sins and turn away from
evil," was his message, "so you can enter
God's Kingdom, which is nearly here!"

John was such a powerful speaker that
people travelled especially to see him.
People from all walks of life flocked from
towns, villages and the city of Jerusalem too.
From poor common people, to powerful
Jewish groups such as the Pharisees and the
Sadducees, as well as farmers, shop keepers,
tax collectors and even Roman soldiers.
They usually found John on the banks of
the River Jordan.

"What does God want from us?" they
would ask.

John would advise, "Be kind and generous. Treat each other fairly. Don't hurt anyone, neither in your actions nor words."

John's teachings were so stirring that people often asked him if he was the saviour – the Messiah spoken of in the ancient writings. "No," John would insist, "but I am trying to prepare the way for His coming."

One after the other, people would tell John all the things they had done wrong in their lives, hanging their heads in shame. They felt truly sorry for their sins and promised they wouldn't do them again, and that they would turn to God and try to live by His rules. Then John baptized them in the holy river. He dipped the people into

the water and gave them God's blessing, so
their sins were washed away and they could
begin afresh. "I'm only baptizing you
with water," John told them, "but
the man who is coming will baptize
you with the fire of the Holy Spirit.
He is so holy that I am not even good
enough to undo his sandals."

One day, among the crowd on the
banks of the Jordan, Jesus was
waiting to be baptized. John knew
who He was immediately. "It's not
right that I baptize you," John told Jesus.
"You should be baptizing me."

But Jesus insisted that it was what God
wanted. So together the men walked into
the river. As soon as John had baptized Jesus,

the clouds above them parted and light
blaze down on Jesus. A dove came gliding
down and hovered above Jesus, and
John knew that it was
God's Holy Spirit
coming down to
Him. Then a voice
spoke into
everyone's minds
saying, "This is
my beloved son,
with whom I am
very pleased."

Matthew chapter 3;
Mark chapter 1; Luke chapter 3;
John chapter 1

Jesus is Tempted

Jesus went into the desert lands of Judea so He could think undisturbed about God and what He wanted Him to do. Jesus was all alone except for the wild animals. He prayed for forty days and forty nights, until He was weak with tiredness and hunger. Then the devil came to Jesus in His thoughts, trying to tempt Him into committing a sin.

"If you really are the Son of God," said the devil, "turn these stones into bread."

But Jesus refused to do so. He had heard God call Him His son when John baptized Him. He didn't need to work a miracle to prove it, and He knew it would be wrong to do so just to make life easier. Even though Jesus felt like fainting through hunger, He trusted God to look after him.

The devil was angry, and he tried again. He made Jesus feel as though He was standing on the roof of the great temple in Jerusalem, looking down on the bustling courtyards below. "Announce to everyone that you are the Son of God," the devil said, "then throw yourself off. The angels will surely catch you!"

But Jesus refused to do so again. He knew it would be wrong to test God in this way. And God wanted to win followers because people loved Him, not just because they'd seen a miracle.

The devil was bursting with fury but he refused to give up. He tried for a third time to get Jesus to sin. The devil made Jesus feel as if He was standing on top of a very high mountain. When He looked down He could see all the countries of the world spread out beneath Him.

"Look," whispered the devil in Jesus' ear. "This is what I can give you – all the lands and peoples from one end of the Earth to the other – if you will just bow down and worship me."

Jesus knew that a lot of people had turned to wickedness in order to make themselves powerful rulers. But the kingdoms the devil helped them establish were full of cruelty and misery. Moreover, Jesus knew that only one kingdom would last forever – the Kingdom of God.

"No! Get away from me!" roared Jesus.
"I will only worship God."

The devil was defeated and he crept
away. As Jesus sank down, utterly exhausted,
angels came to look after Him.

Matthew chapter 4; Mark chapter 1; Luke chapter 4

Jesus' First Miracle

Jesus left the River Jordan and the desert lands of Judea in the south behind Him and went back to live in Galilee in the north. He knew God wanted Him to begin teaching everyone what they had to do to enter His Kingdom. Several followers of John the Baptist went with Jesus to help.

Jesus preached in Jewish places of worship called synagogues. "Beg God to forgive your sins," He told everyone, just like John the Baptist had, "so you can enter the Kingdom of God, which is coming." News soon spread that Jesus was an exciting speaker and He quickly built a following.

Not long after Jesus had arrived back in Galilee, His mother Mary told Him that they had been invited to a wedding in Cana. It was to be a big event and the wedding celebrations were set to go on for several days.

Sitting down at the feast for the wedding everyone was having a wonderful time. About halfway through, Mary noticed that the wine was starting to run out. She knew it would be highly embarrassing for the bride and bridegroom if they couldn't offer their guests any more to drink. So she whispered to Jesus, feeling sure that He could help.

"I'm sorry but I can't do anything about it," Jesus whispered back. "It's not a good time right now."

But Mary turned to the flustered servants and said, "I've noticed that you are low on wine, but my son can help. Do exactly what He says."

Jesus sighed. He gave his mother a gentle smile. Then He told the servants, "Fill all the empty wine jars up to the brim with water." They hurried to do as He said. "Now pour some into a goblet and take it to your boss, the steward, for tasting," Jesus instructed. They did so, rather worried, but to their astonishment the steward smacked his lips, clapped his hands and ordered it to be served to the guests at once. The water had turned into wine. Not only that, but excellent wine – better than they had previously been serving. The steward strode straight over to the bridegroom to congratulate him on his good taste and generosity.

Through the power of God His Father, Jesus had performed His first miracle. There were many more to come.

Matthew chapter 4; Mark chapter 1; Luke chapter 4; John chapters 1, 2

Jesus Goes Fishing

Jesus sailed out on the Sea of Galilee in a boat belonging to two of His followers, Peter and Andrew who were fishermen. "Throw your nets into the water. Let's see if there are any fish today," Jesus suggested.

"We already know there aren't," Peter replied gloomily. "We were fishing all last

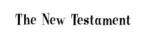

night and we didn't catch a thing."

"Well, why not try again?" Jesus urged.

"I don't think there's much point," Peter shrugged. Then he saw a strange gleam in Jesus' eyes. "But I suppose there's no harm in having another go."

He and Andrew lowered their nets and waited… Then after a while, the brothers went to lift them up again. To their astonishment, the nets were so heavy with fish that they couldn't raise them. The stunned pair had to signal for help from a nearby boat, belonging to the two sons of a man called Zebedee. Their names were James and John and they rowed over to help.

Jesus watched the four men work hard together. It took all their strength to heave

the enormous catch aboard. Soon Peter
and Andrew's little boat was full of shiny,
wriggling fish, and so weighed down in the
water that it was in danger of sinking.

The men knew that this sort of catch was unheard of. Something miraculous must have happened. Peter fell on his knees before Jesus and said, "Lord, I'm not good enough to be one of your followers. I shouldn't have doubted what you said, I should have just done it straight away."

"Don't worry," Jesus said, kindly. "Anyway, I'm going to show you how to catch people instead of fish…"

From then on, Peter, Andrew, James and John stayed at Jesus' side and helped him.

Matthew chapter 4; Mark chapter 1; Luke chapter 5

Wonders at Capernaum

Worshippers in synagogues who heard Jesus preach were always amazed at the way He spoke. Jesus didn't just read out the ancient holy writings as most Jewish teachers did, He actually explained them.

One day, Jesus was in the synagogue at Capernaum, in the middle of giving a speech, when a man burst out of the crowd around Him and started shouting wildly. "I know who you are!" he yelled, pointing his finger threateningly in Jesus' face. "You're a messenger from God. And I know what you've been sent to do, you have come to destroy us all!"

As the crowd gasped in shock, Jesus remained calm. "Be quiet," He commanded. Then He shut his eyes and after a moment said sternly, "Leave him alone!"

All at once the man fainted and crumpled to the floor. When he recovered, he seemed to be a completely different person. He was quiet and calm, if somewhat confused. There had been demons inside the man, but Jesus had ordered them out.

All those who witnessed this incredible event couldn't believe their eyes and ears. Who is this Jesus of Nazareth they wondered? What sort of strange powers does He have that He is able to command demons?

Meanwhile, Jesus had gone to Peter's house. Peter told Him that his mother-in-law was very ill with an extremely high temperature and begged Jesus to visit her to see if He could help. Jesus stood by the bedside of the sick woman who was shivering and sweating with fever, and groaning in pain. Jesus took her hand and said simply but firmly, "Be well." Straight away the hot flush seemed to fade from her cheeks. She stopped writhing around and her breathing calmed. Then she opened her eyes, looked around at everyone and said, "What am I doing in bed? Peter, you should have told me we had guests. Now what would everyone like to eat and drink?" And she got up and began bustling around.

News of what happened at the synagogue and at Peter's house spread around Capernaum and the surrounding towns in no time. Before sunset, there was a long queue outside Peter's door, everyone wanting to see Jesus. People had come from miles around, begging to be cured of all sorts of illnesses. They had brought their sick relations and friends with them too.

Very patiently, Jesus saw them all, one by one. Before the night had ended, He had placed his hands upon every single person and they had all been cured.

Jesus left Capernaum early next morning, so as not to cause a fuss. But as soon as the

grateful townspeople realized he had gone, they tracked Him down and begged Him to stay. "I'm afraid I can't," Jesus insisted.

"People in other places need me. I have to tell everyone how they can find happiness by turning to God. It is what I have been sent to do." And He and His followers, called disciples, went on their way.

Matthew chapters 7, 8; Luke chapter 4

Jesus
the Healer

Soon people from far and wide came to hear about Jesus. Men, women and children were excited by the sound of this captivating preacher who worked miracles. They began seeking Jesus out, travelling to wherever He was to see Him for themselves. Jesus tried to help as many people as He could and convince them to turn to God.

After Jesus had preached in one place, a man who was suffering from the terrible skin disease leprosy crept up to Him. He was extremely nervous about approaching Jesus. Leprosy was very contagious and also incurable, and most people didn't want lepers anywhere near them. In fact, people usually ran away when they saw a leper coming. But Jesus didn't. The poor man knelt before Him, his skin misshapen and ugly with sores, and said, "I know that you can cure me, if you want to."

"Of course I want to," Jesus murmured, and He reached out and placed His hand on the leper's crumbling skin.

It took a couple of moments for the leper

to recover from the shock. After all, most people wouldn't dream of touching him.

But then the man looked at his hands, his legs and felt his face. His skin was healed. He was cured!

"Don't tell anyone," Jesus told the man, who was sobbing his gratitude. "Just go to your priest so he can see for himself and make an offering of thanks to God."

Another time, Jesus shocked many people when He helped an officer in the Roman army. After all, most Jewish people hated the Romans because they had taken control of Israel. The Roman officer begged Jesus to help his servant who was lying ill at home in great pain. "I will come with you straight away," Jesus told the Roman officer.

"That won't be necessary," the Roman insisted. "I know if you just give the word for my servant to recover, he will do so."

Jesus was stunned and delighted. "I haven't met a Jewish person who has shown as much faith as this," He said. "There will be many people from far-off lands who will be able to enter the Kingdom of Heaven, while many from the nation of Israel will be locked outside."

The Roman officer returned home to find his servant completely cured.

Matthew chapter 8; Mark chapter 1; Luke chapter 7; John chapter 4

Jesus Forgives Sins

O ne day Jesus was preaching in a house in Capernaum that was full of people. Many of them were important Jewish people such as officials, priests and Pharisees. These highly regarded elders had travelled from all over Israel to see for themselves the strange preacher everyone was talking about. They

had many questions they wanted answering.
Who was Jesus? Was He a trickster, or a
prophet like Elijah? Was He really the
Messiah spoken of in the ancient holy
books? And what was Jesus teaching? They
didn't want Jesus leading everyone astray.
After all He wasn't even a priest with
training in Jewish holy laws.

There were so many people in the house.
They were jammed shoulder-to-shoulder in
each room and wedged into the hall,
spilling out into the street. Outside there
were many more, straining to hear and get
a glimpse of Jesus through the windows.

While Jesus spoke, four latecomers
staggered up to the house carrying a
paralyzed friend on a stretcher. They were

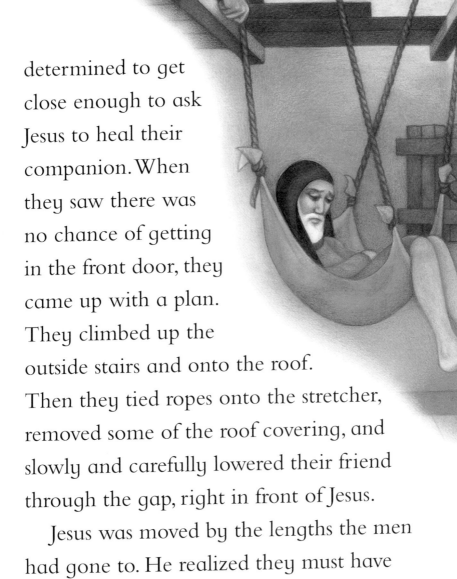

determined to get close enough to ask Jesus to heal their companion. When they saw there was no chance of getting in the front door, they came up with a plan. They climbed up the outside stairs and onto the roof. Then they tied ropes onto the stretcher, removed some of the roof covering, and slowly and carefully lowered their friend through the gap, right in front of Jesus.

Jesus was moved by the lengths the men had gone to. He realized they must have huge faith in Him and great love for their sick friend. He looked down at the suffering man, placed His hand on his head and said, "Take heart, your sins are forgiven."

At His words the room erupted into uproar. The Jewish officials and holy men were outraged. They could believe that Jesus might perhaps have genuine powers of healing, but no one had the power to forgive sins except God Himself. Jesus was committing a terrible sin by saying He could do so. In fact, under Jewish law it was the crime of blasphemy for which He could be severely punished.

Jesus signalled for everyone to calm down and the room gradually fell silent. He asked, "Do you think it's easier for me to say, 'I forgive your sins,' or for me to say,

'Get up off that stretcher, you can now walk'?" The Jewish elders mumbled to each other. Of course it was easier for Jesus to say that He had done something which they couldn't see. Jesus went on, "Maybe you'll believe that God has given me the power to heal this man's soul if I heal his body too."

Jesus looked into the eyes of the man lying stiff and still on his stretcher. "My friend, get up and walk," He said.

To everyone's amazement, he did. The Jewish officials and holy men left the house with more new questions than answers.

Matthew chapter 9; Mark chapter 2; Luke chapter 5

Trouble Bubbles

Jesus continued to travel around, stunning people with wise teachings and performing many miracles of healing. He made new friends and won followers every day, but He made enemies too. People in Jesus' home town of Nazareth were annoyed by how famous He was becoming.

As far as they were concerned, Jesus was just the son of Joseph, the local carpenter – an ordinary person just like them. What could He possibly know about God? How could He work miracles? They sneered and turned their backs on Him.

Jesus often offended Jewish officials and religious leaders too. They had spent their lives studying ancient holy writings and working out what they meant. Now Jesus was preaching about them in new, exciting ways. He even dared to say that Jewish holy men, such as the Pharisees who followed strict laws, had got things wrong. For instance, Jewish law taught that some foods were 'unclean' and shouldn't be eaten. But Jesus said, "It isn't what goes into us that is unclean, it's what comes out of us such as wicked thoughts and deeds." He also announced, "The Pharisees believe that washing in certain ways cleanses your soul. But it doesn't, it only cleanses your body." When Jesus spoke against the Jewish holy men like this, it made them angry.

What made them even more furious was that in their eyes, Jesus often broke rules about the holy seventh day of the week, the Sabbath. Jewish holy books said that God had commanded everyone to rest on the Sabbath. But Jesus often performed miracles, which the Jewish leaders considered to be work. One Sabbath, Jesus healed a crippled woman who had been in terrible pain for eighteen years. On another Sabbath he cured a man with a paralyzed hand.

"Don't you think it's right that we should help people on God's holy day?" Jesus challenged anyone who objected. "My Father doesn't stop working on the Sabbath, and neither do I."

Then the Jewish leaders were completely enraged. "How dare He call God His Father!" they gasped. Many of the officials, priests and Pharisees began plotting ways to get rid of Jesus.

Matthew chapters 12, 13, 15; Mark chapters 3, 6, 7;
Luke chapters 4, 6, 13; John chapters 5, 6

Jesus Befriends Outcasts

One day Jesus was walking down a street with many of his disciples. He peered through a window and saw a man called Matthew busy working at a desk in the tax office. Jesus thought how lonely he looked. He realized that Matthew must have very few friends, if any at all. He was working as a tax collector for the Romans who were ruling Israel, and Jewish people hated the Romans. They wanted them out of their country. Tax collectors were seen to be working for the enemy.

Jesus took pity on Matthew. "Come with me," He said, with a kind smile.

Matthew felt he simply had to do as he was told. He got up, leaving his work exactly as it was, and went off with Jesus and His followers.

After that, Matthew didn't want to lose his kind, new friend. When it grew late in the day, Matthew insisted that Jesus should be his guest for supper. He invited some of the other workers from the tax office too. His usually quiet little house was filled with the happy sound of people chatting over an enjoyable meal.

Of course, when the local Pharisees heard what was going on, they didn't like it one bit. "Jesus should be sitting down to eat with important, holy people like us," they grumbled, "not common folk – and shameful traitors too!"

But Jesus explained, "I haven't come to befriend only good people. In fact, it's sinners who need me the most."

Jesus once went to dinner at the house of a Pharisee, and He wasn't very impressed. The man, called Simon, didn't give him a warm welcome at all. It was good manners for a host to greet his guests with a kiss, and give them some perfume to refresh themselves with. It was also usual for a host to give guests some water and towels so they (or a servant) could wash the dust off their feet. Simon the Pharisee did none of these things for Jesus.

However, during the meal, a woman crept into the room who had lived a very sinful life. Other people thought she was shameful and wouldn't have anything to do with her. But now, the woman knelt before Jesus and begged for forgiveness, sobbing quietly. Her falling tears wet Jesus' feet, and she used her long hair to dry them. Then she soothed them with some expensive perfume that she had brought.

"See," Jesus said to Simon the Pharisee, "you think of yourself as a holy man and this woman as sinful, but she has shown me every kindness that you have not. It doesn't matter at all that she has done wrong in the past, she is now truly sorry and her sins are all forgiven."

And the woman went home with joy in her heart, determined to follow Jesus and live a good life from then on.

Matthew chapter 9; Mark chapter 2; Luke chapters 5, 7

Jesus Chooses Special Helpers

Jesus became so well known that He couldn't go anywhere without being surrounded by crowds. He once climbed high up a mountain so He could be on His own. Jesus prayed to God all night. When He came down the next day, He summoned twelve men from His many disciples.

They were brothers Peter and Andrew, brothers James and John, a former follower of John the Baptist called Philip, Matthew the tax collector, a man called Simon who was a member of a Jewish group called the Zealots, a second James, and four others – Thomas, Bartholomew, Thaddaeus and Judas Iscariot.

Jesus took the twelve men to one side and spoke to them. "I want you to be my special helpers," He explained. "I want each of you to go and preach to people what I have preached. I am going to give you the power to heal the sick, just as I do. Don't accept any money for it. Don't take anything on your travels except for the clothes you are wearing, just live off people's kindness. It won't be easy – some people will ignore you, others will try to stop you spreading my message and some may even try to have you killed. But God will always be with you, looking after you, and His Holy Spirit will give you courage. And if you give up your life for me, I promise you will have a new and happier life in Heaven."

So for several weeks, the twelve men went out around the countryside, teaching and healing in Jesus' name.

Matthew chapter 10; Mark chapters 3, 6; Luke chapters 6, 9

The Sermon
on the Mount

One day a vast crowd gathered to hear Jesus speak, so He went up a hillside so that everyone could see and hear Him.

"Blessed are all those who realize that God is missing from their lives," He preached, "for they will one day enter Heaven. Blessed are all sad people, for they will be comforted. Blessed are gentle people, for all the Earth will be theirs. Blessed are those who try to live good lives, for they will be well rewarded. Blessed are those who take pity on others, for they will be shown pity too. Blessed are those with pure hearts, for they will see God. Blessed are those who work for peace, for God cares for them as His own children. Blessed are those who follow God but are made to suffer because of it – the Kingdom of Heaven will belong to them. I want you all to follow my teachings even if people make it difficult for you. I want you to be like a light, showing others the right way."

Everyone was quiet and listening so hard, you could almost hear the plants growing.

"Don't think that I am telling you to forget about the old religious teachings and rules," Jesus went on. "I'm telling you to pay more attention to them than ever. You've been told that it is a sin to kill anyone. I'm telling you that you should not even argue with anyone. You've been told that you should not take something that belongs to someone else just because you want it. I'm telling you that you shouldn't even think about it in the first place. You've been told that if someone is nasty to you, it's alright to get your own back. I'm telling you that you should forget it and do nothing. You should treat your enemies the same as you treat your friends. And don't hoard riches and luxuries on Earth where they can be

stolen or destroyed. Instead think of good
deeds as coins, and try to stack them up. But
don't boast – God knows everything
anyway. Lastly, don't worry about everyday
things such as how you are going to pay for
food to eat or clothes to wear. If you put
your energy into looking for God,
He will look after you in turn."

Then Jesus told everyone how to pray. "Go somewhere quiet where you can be alone," He said, "and talk to God directly, as if you were talking to a friend. Just say whatever is in your heart. If there is anything you need, ask Him for it and He will give it to you." And he taught them a special prayer beginning with the words 'Our Father'.

Jesus gave a sad smile. "If you do as I say, you will be like a wise man who builds his home on rock and it will stand firm. But if you take no notice, you will be like a fool who builds his home on sand. The wind will blow it down and the rain will wash it away, until the house is in ruins."

Matthew chapters 5 to 7; Luke chapters 6, 11

Jesus Calms the Storm

Jesus had been preaching to a huge crowd by the Sea of Galilee all day. Evening began drawing in and He felt exhausted. Jesus needed to escape the masses people and rest. "Let's sail to the other side of the lake," He said to a few of his disciples. They all climbed into a boat, pushed off from the shore and raised the sail.

Soon the little boat was speeding across the waters in the setting sun. Jesus sat back, his head drooped and he nodded off, lulled to sleep by the rise and fall of the sea.

While Jesus lay dreaming, the disciples were alarmed to see black clouds overhead. The wind rose, stirring up the water. The disciples hurried to roll up the sail as the gale grew stronger. It whisked the waves up into great peaks, which sent the boat rearing up and then plunging down. Water crashed over the sides. Despite their efforts to bail out the water, the waves kept breaking in, threatening to sink the boat.

Amazingly Jesus slept through it all. But now the terrified disciples woke him.

"Master!" they shouted, struggling to make their voices heard over the wailing winds. "Master, we're all going to drown!"

Jesus opened his eyes and got to his feet. His hair and clothes whipped around him as he stretched out his hands, looked up to the skies and cried, "Be still!"

At once the wind dropped, the waves died away and the clouds faded. All was peaceful again.

But now the disciples were frightened for a new reason. What kind of man could command the wind and the waves?

Matthew chapter 8; Mark chapter 4; Luke chapter 8

Jesus Teaches through Stories

Jesus often preached about God and the way to happiness in Heaven by telling people stories with hidden meanings, called parables. He once told a parable about a farmer who was sowing seed in his field. As he went, he scattered seed all around him so it would grow.

"Some of the seed fell onto the footpath," said Jesus, "so it didn't sink into the soil and birds swooped down and ate it up. These seeds never had a chance to grow."

Jesus went on, "Other seeds fell onto rocky, stony ground. They started to grow, but couldn't put down deep, strong roots. Under the hot summer sun, the young crops couldn't take up enough moisture from the earth and they withered, scorched and died."

Jesus continued, "Some seeds landed on patches of thorny weeds. The crops grew but the weeds grew up faster and choked them. However, some seeds fell onto good, rich soil and they grew into tall, plentiful crops."

Jesus didn't tell His listeners what the parable meant. He wanted them to try to understand it for themselves. That way, they would really think about what Jesus had told them and they wouldn't forget His message.

Later Jesus explained to His disciples. "The seed is the Word of God. The footpath stands for people who hear the Word of God but who don't take it in. The devil will swoop down and seize it from them so they forget. The seed that falls on rocky ground stands for people who listen to the Word of God but don't take it in. When they are faced with problems, their difficulties overcome them. The seed that falls among weeds stands for people who hear the Word of God but get distracted by selfish habits and desires. Finally, the seed that falls onto good soil stands for people who take the Word of God into their hearts. Over time it grows there and bears fruit."

Jesus warned everyone to listen hard to His parables. "No one buys a lamp and hides its light," he said. "So don't ignore my teachings. Everything I am telling you will one day prove to be true."

Matthew chapter 13; Mark chapter 4; Luke chapter 8

Jesus Wakes
the Dead

One day, a man in great distress came
pushing through the hundreds of
people surrounding Jesus. His name was
Jairus and he was a leader at the local
synagogue. He fell on his knees and begged
Jesus for His help. "Master, my daughter is
dying," he sobbed. "She is only twelve.

Please come to my home, I beg you. I know you can save her and make her well again."

Jesus set off with Jairus immediately and the enormous crowd went with them. As everyone jostled along, they pushed and elbowed each other to get closer to Jesus. Suddenly He stopped and span around.

"Which person touched me?" Jesus demanded, scanning the faces of those surrounding him. Everyone shifted about looking nervous.

"Master," said Peter, "it's such a crush. How can you ask if one particular person touched you? Many people are!"

"No," Jesus insisted. "When one person touched me I felt power go out of me."

His searching eyes landed on a woman

in the crowd who had been ill for twelve
years with a painful disease. She had been
to many doctors but none had been able to
cure her. However she had great faith in
Jesus. She believed that even if she couldn't
speak to Him, if she could only touch Him,
she would be cured. As Jesus walked along
in the jostling crowd, the woman had
pushed as close to Him as she could, then
thrust her arm between the people in front
of her. Her fingertips brushed His robe and
  immediately she was cured.

    She hung her head waiting to be told
off. But Jesus smiled at her gently.

      "Don't be afraid," He said. "Your
faith has cured you."

      All this time Jairus had

been waiting, growing more and more worried that they would reach his house too late to save his daughter. Now his worst fears came true. As they neared Jairus' house one of his servants approached, unable to look him in the eye. "Sir," Jairus' servant said softly, "don't trouble the preacher any further. Your daughter has passed away."

Jesus overheard this. "Don't be afraid," he said to the grief-stricken man. "Trust me. All will be well."

They continued on to Jairus' house to find a group of people already outside, weeping and wailing. "What is all this fuss for?" Jesus protested. "Jairus' daughter isn't dead, she's just in a deep sleep."

Jesus followed Jairus and his heartbroken wife, along with Peter, James and John, into the room where the little girl lay cold and lifeless. He sat beside her on the bed and gently took her hand. "It's time to get up now," Jesus said.

Instantly, the little girl opened her eyes, stretched and got out of bed, straight into the arms of her overjoyed parents.

"Now don't tell anyone about this," Jesus warned Jairus and his wife, who were weeping with joy. But of course they couldn't help telling everyone they knew. The news spread and Jesus' fame became even greater than before.

Matthew chapter 9; Mark chapter 5; Luke chapter 8

The Coming
of the Kingdom

Jesus once told a parable that warned
people they must always be ready for the
coming of the Kingdom of Heaven.

"Imagine the scene at a bride's house
where her wedding is to be held," Jesus said.
"The bride and all her guests are inside,
ready for the ceremony to begin. All they

need is the bridegroom. The bride asks ten friends to wait outside to welcome him in. The girls each hold an oil lamp because it is late and darkness is drawing in.

"The bridegroom takes longer than expected to arrive and the bridesmaids have to stand and wait for a long time. They sit down to rest and soon they all nod off.

"Suddenly the girls are woken by shouting, 'The bridegroom is on his way!' However, the girls find themselves in darkness – the oil in each lamp had burned dry. Five girls have spare oil and they hastily relight their lamps. But the other five girls didn't remember to bring any extra oil.

"'Can we share some of yours?' they ask their friends.

"'We don't have enough to go around,' the sensible girls explain. 'From the sound of that announcement the bridegroom is still quite a way off and if we share, none of our lamps will last long enough. You might have time to buy some more if you hurry.'

"The five forgetful girls dash off to the nearest shop to buy more oil. But while they are gone, the bridegroom arrives. The five waiting girls call the guests out to greet

him and amid joyful singing and dancing
they light his way into the house with their
bright lamps held high.

"By the time the girls arrive back from
the shop with their lamps lit again, the front
door is shut and the wedding party is in full
swing inside. 'We're here!' the foolish girls
call, knocking on the door. 'Open up!'

"But a guest inside calls, 'I'm sorry, I
don't know who you are. I can't let you in.'

"So the girls are left outside in the chilly
night, shut out of the party."

Jesus warned His listeners, "Don't be like
the five forgetful girls. Always be prepared
for God's coming because no one knows
when that moment will arrive."

Matthew chapter 5

The Miracle at the Pool

Jesus once went to Jerusalem to attend an important religious festival. While he was there, he visited a holy pool at a place called Bethesda. The pool was always surrounded by many sick and injured people. They gathered there hoping to bathe in the water and be miraculously cured. It was believed that every so often an angel stirred up the waters and the first person to bathe in the pool when this happened would be healed. Jesus saw one man there who had been crippled for thirty-eight years. Jesus knew that he had been waiting by the pool for a very long time. Whenever the man saw ripples appear on the water, he would struggle to drag himself towards the edge of the pool. But moving was so slow and painful for him that other people always beat him to it. Even on the rare occasion that he made it to the pool first, there was no one to help him get into the water.

Jesus felt great pity for the poor man and greatly admired him for his faith and courage. He decided that the man had waited long enough for a miracle. "Stand up and pick up your mat. You can walk," Jesus said.

And to the man's astonishment and joy, he did so. He went straight to the great temple to give thanks to God, taking delight in each step he took. A group of Jewish leaders were there and recognized him. "But you were crippled!" they marvelled. "Whatever has happened to you?"

"Jesus of Nazareth cured me," the man told them, and explained everything that had happened.

Instead of being pleased, the Jewish leaders were furious. Jesus had worked yet another miracle on the holy day of rest, the Sabbath. Outraged, they grew more determined than ever to get rid of him.

John chapter 5

Two Fish and Five Loaves

There came a time when the King of Judea had John the Baptist, Jesus' good friend, thrown into prison and put to death. When Jesus heard the news, He was preaching at the Sea of Galilee. He was upset and wanted to escape the crowds who followed Him everywhere, so He could be

on His own for a little while. Jesus and His
twelve disciples took a little boat out across
the waters. However, the hundreds of people
who had come to see and hear Jesus raced
around the coast, joined by more people
they met on the way. The crowd was there
waiting for Jesus and His friends when they
arrived on the far shore.

Jesus looked at the great mass of people
– many of them sick or injured, hoping
desperately for a cure. His heart went out to
them. "Look at them," Jesus murmured.
"They are like sheep without a shepherd."

Even though Jesus was grief-stricken and
exhausted, He began preaching and
healing… and was still talking to the people
when dusk began to fall.

"Master, you've done enough now," the disciples said, concerned for Jesus. "It's time everyone went home. We all need something to eat."

Jesus smiled wearily. "No one needs to go anywhere," He said. "You can find us all some dinner."

The disciples looked at each other in confusion. They were surrounded by at least five thousand people. How did Jesus expect the disciples to feed them all?

"We've hardly any money between all of us to buy anything for supper," Philip pointed out.

Andrew added, "The only food we have is what this lad has brought with him," and he indicated a young boy carrying a basket.

"He's got five loaves of bread and two fish, but they'll hardly go very far!"

Jesus stretched out his hands over the

loaves and fish, said a blessing and broke them into pieces. Then He told his disciples, "Now share them out among everyone."

The disciples knew that they should trust Jesus, no matter what. To their amazement, there was enough bread and fish for everybody to have a hearty supper and enough left over to fill twelve baskets.

Matthew chapter 14; Mark chapter 6; Luke chapter 9; John chapter 6

Walking on Water

It had been a long day at the Sea of Galilee. Jesus told his weary disciples to head for home without Him while He sent away the thousands of people who had gathered. "It's going to take a little while for me to convince everyone to leave," Jesus said to His friends with a sigh. "You start off without me. I want to spend some time praying on my own. I'll catch up with you."

"But how will you follow us?" The disciples protested, clambering into their little boats.

"Don't worry, I'll be fine," Jesus reassured, waving them off.

As the men sailed away, Jesus turned back to the crowds and told them it was time to go home too. No one wanted to leave Him, but eventually they began to wander away in groups. At last, Jesus was able to leave unnoticed and went a little way up a hillside. Finally, He had some peace and quiet and could pray alone. He stayed for quite a while, deep in thought, talking to God.

Meanwhile out on the Sea of Galilee, the disciples were in trouble. The wind had grown stronger, stirring up strong currents in the water and battering the little boats. The alarmed men rolled up the sails and tried to row to shore, but despite straining at the oars with all their might, the boats were being blown off course, out into dangerous open waters.

Hours passed and as the night grew darker, the wind grew wilder and the waves grew higher. The disciples realized they were lost at sea and they were terrified.

As they sat huddled in their boats, desperately waiting for the light of dawn, they saw a white glow in the darkness. It came closer and grew bigger, turning into

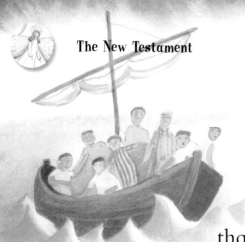

the shape of a man.

"A ghost!" they cried, even more frightened than before. Then a voice came floating towards them on the wind.

"Don't be afraid. It's me, Jesus."

The disciples were confused. Was it really their friend and master? Or was a demon trying to trick them?

Peter spoke up bravely. "If it's really you, Lord," he shouted back, "tell me to walk to you across the waves."

"Yes, come then," Jesus called.

Peter stood up, cautiously moved to the edge of the rocking boat and took a deep breath. The other disciples could hardly believe their eyes as Peter stepped out.

Far from sinking into the churning
waters, their friend strode from wave to
wave, over the swirling sea,
towards Jesus.
Peter kept his
eyes fixed on
Jesus, not
daring to look down.
But when he was
within a couple of steps of
Jesus, his curiosity got the better
of him and he glanced down. The
moment he saw the frothing
foam beneath his feet, his
courage deserted him and he
plunged down into the dark,
cold waters. "Help me, Jesus!"

Peter screamed in a panic. "I'm sinking!"

Jesus reached out and grabbed Peter's hand, heaving him up. "Don't doubt me," He said. "Have more faith." Jesus guided his friend back to the boats and suddenly the wind died down and the waves calmed.

The disciples had watched everything in amazement. "You really are the Son of God," they said, falling in awe at Jesus' feet.

Matthew chapter 14; Mark chapter 6; John chapter 6

The Good Samaritan

Jesus always surprised people by knowing Jewish religious rules inside out and back to front. Many religious leaders and holy men who had spent their whole lives studying the laws were jealous of Jesus' knowledge. So they would ask tricky questions to try to catch Him out.

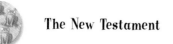

One day a lawyer came to Jesus and asked, "What must I do to win eternal life?"

"What does the law tell you to do?" Jesus answered simply.

"To love God with all my heart and soul, and to love my neighbour as I love myself," the lawyer reeled off smugly, showing off his knowledge.

"Exactly," said Jesus. "If you already know, why are you asking me?"

"Ah, but who is my neighbour?" the man asked, feeling confident that he had posed a question far too difficult for Jesus to answer.

"Let me tell you a story," Jesus said, without a moment's hesitation. "There was once a man travelling on the road from Jerusalem to Jericho. Suddenly a group of bandits sprang out from behind some rocks and attacked him. There was no one around to hear the traveller's cries for help. The bandits beat him, robbed him of all his possessions and left him for dead.

"After a while, a priest came walking down the road," Jesus continued. "He wondered what a bundle of rags was doing in the middle of the road and went over to have a look. As soon as the priest saw that the heap was actually a man lying bleeding in the dust, he quickly crossed to the other side of the road. He didn't want to know what had happened or have anything to do with it."

The lawyer gasped, "How could such a holy man not help someone in need?"

"The next traveller to approach was a Levite," Jesus carried on.

"This man is sure to help," said the Lawyer. Jews from the tribe of Levi were so god-fearing that priests were always chosen from among them.

"The Levite shuddered in disgust when he saw the battered and bruised man barely alive," Jesus continued. "Like the priest before him, he crossed to the far side of the road and walked away."

Now the lawyer was really shocked. A holy Levite should have known better.

"Next, a Samaritan passed by," Jesus announced.

The lawyer pulled a face. Samaritans were the people who had been sent to live in Israel when the Jews were taken away as slaves by the Babylonians. The Jews hated the Samaritans for taking their land. They also looked down on the Samaritans because they weren't God's Chosen People and often didn't worship God at all. The lawyer thought the Samaritan probably went over to see if there was anything left to steal!

But Jesus continued, "The Samaritan was

appalled when he saw the dying man and rushed to help. He gave the poor man some water, heaved him up onto his donkey and hurried to the nearest town. There he paid an innkeeper to take him in and look after him until he was better."

The lawyer was flabbergasted.

"Now which of the three travellers would you say was the neighbour of the attacked man?" Jesus asked.

"The one who helped him," stuttered the lawyer.

"Right," said Jesus. "Now go and behave like the Samaritan."

Luke chapter 10

A Visit to Martha and Mary

Jesus once stopped in a little village called Bethany. A woman called Martha who lived in the village invited Jesus and His disciples into her house to rest and eat. They were grateful and accepted her kind offer.

Martha introduced the men to her sister, Mary. Then she showed Jesus and His

friends to where they could sit, and began
bustling about. First she disappeared into
the kitchen and brought out bowls of water
and towels so that they could freshen up
from the dust of the road. Then she went
to fetch pitchers of juice and drinking
cups to quench their thirst. Back to
the kitchen she dashed to prepare
trays of hot drinks and plates of food.

Meanwhile, Mary had made
herself comfortable at Jesus' feet.
While Martha was racing about,
seeing to their guests, Mary sat and
gazed up at the great preacher,
listening intently to every word He said.

"Mary, it would be nice if you gave me
a hand," Martha whispered, carrying

another tray of food.

But her sister didn't follow her back to the kitchen. Instead, Martha found herself cooking dinner for thirteen guests all on her own. How fed up she felt! After all, she would like to be sitting and chatting with the famous preacher and His twelve friends. But somebody had to prepare the food, and her sister wasn't going to do it.

So Martha continued to make trips back and forth from the kitchen, carrying in starters, main courses and desserts, and clearing away tray after tray of empty plates, bowls and cups.

By the time everyone had finished eating and Martha had cleared everything away, Jesus, the disciples and Mary were deep in conversation. Martha had missed the start of the discussion so she couldn't really understand what they were talking about. And her guests had all spread out so much in the room that there was hardly space for her to sit down.

How left out Martha felt! As she looked at her sister sitting right next to Jesus, having done nothing at all, she felt a lump rise in her throat and tears begin to prick her eyes.

"Lord," she suddenly burst out in frustration, "how could you let my sister just sit there lazily and do nothing? Why didn't you tell her to get up and help?"

"My poor Martha, thank you so much for your kindness," Jesus said, getting up to comfort the upset woman. "But you have prepared so many different dishes for us when just one would have been enough. Your sister has chosen to pay attention to me in the best way of all – listening. I can't possibly tell her off for that."

Luke chapter 10

A Story of Forgiveness

Jesus told a story about a farmer who had two sons. The farmer was teaching his sons all about farming so that when he died, they could take over. However one day, the younger son approached his father with an idea.

"I've been thinking, father," he said

nervously. "I'm grown up and it's time I saw a bit of the world. It would help if I could have my share of the farm now in cash."

The farmer loved his sons dearly and he didn't even have to think about the decision. He counted hundreds of silver coins into bags and handed them to the excited lad.

"Thank you, father," he said, packing his bags to set off. "You won't regret it."

And the farmer watched with tears in his eyes as his younger son left home.

For a while the farmer's son had a wonderful time. He lived like a prince, visiting the finest cities, eating out every night and going to parties. He was surrounded by people who wanted to be his friend, but the problem was they helped him spend all his money. When the silver was gone, his friends vanished too. The young man found himself alone and far from home, without even a few pennies to buy a loaf of bread. To make matters worse, a dreadful drought swept through the land, causing a terrible famine. The farmer's son couldn't even beg for food because no one had enough for themselves. Luckily, he found a job as a pig-keeper. But the wages were pitiful. He had hardly enough money left to buy food after paying his rent. Some days he was so hungry he nearly ate the food for the pigs!

One day, he decided enough was enough. "I want to go home," he groaned. "I'll beg my father for his forgiveness for being such an idiot. He's bound to be furious, but maybe if I grovel, he'll let me stay and work as one of his farm labourers."

The miserable, ragged young man arrived home and couldn't believe how overjoyed his father was to see him. "I've worried about you and missed you every day, son," the farmer cried, hugging and kissing him.

The ashamed son sobbed as he told his father what had happened.

"Never mind," the farmer said, to his

son's utter astonishment. "You're back home now and we're together again. That's all that matters."

Later, the farmer's elder son came home from a hard day's work in the fields to find a party in full swing. The neighbours had been invited over to celebrate, and a feast had been prepared. There was music, dancing and the people were drinking wine.

"Whatever's going on here?" he gasped, and one of the servants explained what had happened.

The farmer swung his elder son round in a jig. "Rejoice!" he cried. "Your little brother has finally come back home!"

"What do you mean, 'rejoice'?" the elder son spat, completely furious. "I've stayed with you all these years, working my fingers to the bone, and you've never given me so much as a thank you – let alone thrown me a party! Then HE turns up, having wasted most of your fortune, and you're celebrating how wonderful he is!"

"You have no idea how much your faithfulness means to me," the farmer said to his elder son, drawing him close in a hug. "Everything I have, I give to you. But today is a day to be glad, for your brother was lost and gone forever, but he has come home."

Luke chapter 15

The Pharisee and the Tax Collector

T he Pharisees were Jews who had been brought up to live according to strict religious rules. They believed that their ways of living were the right ways – the only ways – and everyone who didn't follow their rules were not as good as them.

However, Jesus often warned the

Pharisees that they were committing all sorts of sins without realizing it. One was the sin of looking down on others, and He told this story to try to make the Pharisees think about it.

"Two men went into the temple to pray. One was a Pharisee," the Pharisees in the crowd of listeners all smiled smugly, "and one was a tax collector," people booed and hissed at the thought of the traitors who worked for the Romans. "The Pharisee strode straight into the middle of the temple," Jesus continued, "in full view of the people around. He lifted his arms, raised his eyes to the heavens and prayed in a loud, confident voice so that everyone could clearly hear him. 'Thank you, O God,' he said, 'for making me better than common sinners. Thank you for not making me a liar or a cheat like most people. Thank you for giving me the strength to fast twice a week and the generosity to give part of everything I earn to charity. Thank you for not making me like that greedy tax collector over there.'

"The tax collector was lurking behind a pillar in the shadows, trying his best not to be noticed by anyone. He knelt and bowed his head low, whispering, 'Lord, I am a sinner. I ask for forgiveness, even though I am not worthy of your mercy.'

"Now," finished Jesus, "That day it was the tax collector who went home with God's blessing. For those who set themselves up high will one day fall, and those who think of themselves as lowly will one day be raised up."

Of course the Pharisees didn't like that particular story one little bit.

Luke chapter 18

Jesus and the Children

The twelve disciples were travelling with Jesus along a road one day. They began to fall behind, squabbling among themselves. Their argument was about which of them would be the greatest in the Kingdom of Heaven. They thought that Jesus couldn't hear them, but He did. They were saying things like, "Well, I should be the greatest because I'm Jesus' oldest friend…" And, "I should be the greatest because I've performed the most miracles…" And, "No, I'm sure I'll be the greatest because I pray the most often."

Jesus didn't stop them, He just listened to every word. But later on when they had reached their destination and sat down to rest, He asked, "So what were you all talking about on the road then?"

The disciples felt embarrassed to think that Jesus had heard them trying to outdo each other. No one admitted a thing, but Jesus knew all about what had gone on. "If you really want to be the greatest in God's eyes, you must put others before yourself,"

He told the red-faced men. Jesus reached out to a little girl who was passing by and drew her towards Him. "You must be like this child," He said. "You must have simple, honest values and take genuine delight in helping others. Never look down on children, for they are selfless and giving. They are among the greatest in Heaven."

However, it didn't take long for the disciples to forget what Jesus had told them. A few weeks later, Jesus had been preaching all day long when a group of people with young children approached, asking Him to bless them. Some of the children clung to their parents, while others were playful and pestered Jesus for attention. Jesus' disciples were sure that this would be annoying for the weary preacher and they began to shoo the children away. But Jesus stopped his friends. "Let the children come to me," He instructed. "After all, the Kingdom of Heaven belongs to them." Jesus picked up the smallest child and let others scramble onto his lap, blessing them all. "Unless you are pure and wholehearted like these children," He warned his disciples once more, "you will never see God."

Matthew chapters 18, 19;
Mark chapters 9, 10;
Luke chapters 9, 18

403

Jesus the Good Shepherd

Jesus once said to a crowd that had gathered to hear him speak, "What would a shepherd do if wolves attacked the sheep in his flock? If he was a hired shepherd, doing his job only for the money, he wouldn't stay and fight off the wolves. He would run away and save himself, leaving the sheep to be eaten. I am not like that shepherd, I am the good shepherd. I will look after my sheep even if it means I have to die for them. I have flocks in other places too, which I need to gather so I can look after all my animals together. My sheep know my voice, they will listen to me and follow me anywhere. It's because I will give up my life for my sheep willingly – for love, not any other reward – that God loves me and will give me my life back again."

Many of Jesus' listeners were bemused by these words. "He must be mad," some of them mumbled. "Do you think it's demons inside Him that are talking?"

But others knew that Jesus was trying to get them to understand something important. "Of course He's not mad!" they insisted, even though they weren't sure what Jesus meant. "How could someone possessed by demons miraculously heal people?"

What Jesus wanted everyone to know was that He genuinely cared for them. Not just for Jewish people, but for people everywhere who wanted to follow God. He was also warning that He was ready to die for everybody, if that is what He had to do. Jesus was explaining that it is only by loving everyone and willingly helping other people in this world, that God will reward us with new life in the next.

John chapter 10

Lazarus
is Awoken

Amessenger brought urgent news to Jesus from Martha and Mary, the two women he had stayed with in the village of Bethany. Their brother, Lazarus, had fallen seriously ill and they feared he was dying.

Jesus had made firm friends with the two sisters and their brother, and was fond of them. But to the disciples' surprise He didn't rush off when He received the message. "Lazarus will be fine," Jesus told them. "God has made him ill on purpose in order to show His glorious power through me."

Jesus stayed where He was, preaching and healing for another two days. On the third day He told the disciples that He was at last heading back to Bethany. "I have to wake Lazarus," He explained.

"But master," protested the disciples, rather puzzled, "if Lazarus is sleeping, won't he wake up on his own?"

"Lazarus is dead," Jesus announced calmly. "And I am glad I wasn't there to save him because now I can work a miracle that will give you more faith in me."

By the time Jesus arrived at Bethany Lazarus had been dead for four days. As he approached the sisters' house, a red-eyed Martha came out. "Oh Lord," she sobbed, "if only you had been here, Lazarus would not have died." Wiping her tears, she looked at Jesus. "But I know that God will grant you anything you ask for," she whispered.

Jesus was moved by Martha's faith. Holding her gaze, He asked, "Do you accept that anyone who believes in me and dies will live again? That anyone who believes in me and lives will never die?"

"I do, my Lord," replied Martha.

"Then fetch your sister and show me where you have buried your brother," Jesus said gently.

Martha hurried to fetch Mary, and together they and their grief-stricken friends accompanied Jesus to Lazarus' tomb. He had been laid to rest in a cave with a large stone set across the entrance.

"Roll away the rock," Jesus ordered.

The sisters were shocked. "But master, he has been dead for four days," said Martha. "His body will smell."

Jesus waved away their protests. As everyone helped clear the entrance, He started to pray. "Father, you always hear me and answer me," Jesus said, "and I thank you with all my heart. Now I am asking for something that will help everyone believe that it's you who have sent me."

Jesus shut his eyes and stood very still.

Then his firm, clear voice echoed into the cave. "Lazarus, come out!" He commanded.

After a while, everyone heard a shuffling sound and a shrouded figure came staggering out of the cave.

"Don't be afraid, unwrap your brother," Jesus urged Mary and Martha.

Hardly daring to breathe, they did so. Lazarus was alive and well again.

John chapters 11 to 27

Bartimaeus,
the Blind Beggar

Bartimaeus had been a blind beggar in Jericho for as long as anyone could remember. No one knew how old he was, probably not even Bartimaeus himself, but everyone knew who he was. He could always be found sitting in the same spot by the roadside. His begging bowl set on the ground in front of him, and lifting his poor, dull eyes hopefully to each passer-by.

One day Bartimaeus became aware of quite a fuss building around him. "What's going on?" he asked. "Why are there so many people around?"

"Jesus of Nazareth is coming this way," someone replied.

At once, Bartimaeus' heart began to beat faster. He had heard many stories about the great preacher – how He had given the gift of sight to hundreds of blind people just like him. Jesus had healed paralyzed people, cured the lame, made the sick well again. It was rumoured that Jesus had even brought people back from the dead.

As the crowds bustled around the beggar,

he stumbled to his feet and added his voice to theirs. "Jesus! Have pity on me!" he shouted as loud as he could.

"Be quiet, Bartimaeus! Shut up!"came voices from around him. "Jesus is coming and we want to hear what he is saying."

But that just encouraged old Bartimaeus to shout even louder. "Jesus of Nazareth! Help me!" he bellowed, with a strength he didn't know he had. "I'm over here. Please take pity on me!"

Suddenly, the commotion all around him fell silent and he felt a hand on his shoulder.

"My friend, I'm here," came a soft voice. "How would you like me to help you?"

Trembling, Bartimaeus gasped, "Oh Lord, please let me see."

The ragged man felt gentle fingertips touch his eyelids. Then all at once the darkness before him began to lighten and brighten until he could make out blurs… then shapes and colours… He could see! The world was unimaginably beautiful, and Bartimaeus looked at Jesus' smiling face.

"Your faith has made you well," Jesus said, and Bartimaeus followed Him, dancing in celebration along the road.

Matthew chapter 20; Mark chapter 10; Luke chapter 18

The Parable of the Lost Coins

Despite everything Jesus had told His followers, there were many people who thought that He was going to establish God's Kingdom by forming an army and marching against the Romans. Jesus knew that He wasn't going to win any earthly revolution. In fact, He was going to be arrested, put on trial and then executed. The Kingdom of Heaven would come at the end of the world, after Judgement Day, and only God knew when that would be. So Jesus told a parable that he hoped would help people make the most of everything God had given them, while they were waiting.

"There was once a prince who had to travel far away to lay claim to a kingdom that was rightfully his," Jesus began. "Before he went, he called his three most trusted servants and asked them to look after his property while he was away. To the first servant he gave five bags of gold. To the second servant he gave two bags and to the third servant he gave one bag. 'Use my money wisely and well,' he bade them.

"The prince left and years passed. Eventually he returned, now a great king. 'What did you do with my gold,' he asked his servants.

"The first servant traded with his five bags of gold and earned five more. The king was delighted and made him governor of ten of his new cities.

"The second servant had saved his two bags of gold in a bank, where it had doubled with interest making four bags. The king was pleased and made him governor of five new cities.

"The last servant had
hidden his bag of gold
in the ground. 'You
mean to say you
did nothing with
my gift?' the king
roared furiously.
'You made no
use of it at all?' He
turned to his guards.
'Take this man's gold
and then throw him out,' he
commanded. 'Give the gold to the servant
who already has ten bags. For those who
try hard will be rewarded, while those who
do not will lose what little they have.'

Matthew chapter 25; Luke chapter 19

Jesus Warns of the Future

There came a rare moment when Jesus found Himself alone with His disciples, walking along a road. He took the opportunity to talk with them. "I sometimes call myself 'the Son of Man'," He began. "What do you think I mean by that?"

"Some people believe you are John the

Baptist," one disciple shrugged.

"Or the prophet Elijah come back from the dead," another suggested.

"Or a new, greater prophet," a third said.

"But who do you think I am?" He asked.

"I think you are the Messiah, the Son of the Living God," Peter announced firmly.

"Then God has blessed you," Jesus said to Peter. "Your name means 'rock', and you are the rock on which I will build my church. I will give you the keys to Heaven, and whatever rules you set on Earth will also stand in Heaven."

Jesus turned to everyone and said gravely, "I must warn you all that things are soon going to get very difficult. The time is drawing near when I must go to Jerusalem.

I will go through much suffering," Jesus
gave a sigh. "And eventually I will be put to
death." The disciples gasped, but Jesus held
up his hands to silence them. "However,
three days later, I will come back to life."
The disciples were amazed.

"Are you ready to follow me into
hardship and sorrow – even to die for
me?" Jesus asked
his friends. "If you
are, I cannot grant
you a reward in this
world, but I can promise you
joy in the next."

Jesus' friends walked on with
heavy, but determined, hearts.

Matthew chapter 16; Mark chapter 8; Luke chapter 9

Jesus Shows Himself in Glory

One week had passed since Jesus told his disciples that He was the Messiah and warned them of the troubles to come. Now He asked Peter, James and John to go with Him up a hillside a little way to a quiet place where they could pray away from everyone else.

The four men were soon deep in prayer, unaware of anything else around them. But suddenly something made Peter, James and John stop talking to God and turn to look at Jesus. They were shocked to see their kneeling friend so transfixed in prayer. His body looked still and lifeless like a statue, as if His spirit had left it. Jesus' face began to glow brighter and brighter, and His clothes glared whiter and whiter, until He was surrounded by a blaze of glory. It hurt their eyes to look at Him, so they shielded them with their hands. Two other gleaming figures appeared whom they recognized as the great prophets, Moses and Elijah. They listened as Jesus discussed with them what He would have to face in Jerusalem, including His own death.

Then suddenly a towering black cloud surged overhead. "This is my Son, the Chosen One. Listen to Him!" boomed a mighty voice. The disciples were terrified.

When they looked up again, everything had returned to normal. "Don't tell anyone what you have seen," Jesus commanded, "until I have died and risen from the dead."

Matthew chapter 17; Mark chapter 9; Luke chapter 9

The First
Palm Sunday

It was the week before the great feast of
Passover. Jews from far-off lands travelled
to Jerusalem for the celebrations, which
lasted several days. Jewish holy men such as
the chief priests and Pharisees were waiting
to see if Jesus would dare visit the city too.
They had been plotting for a long time to

arrest and execute the preacher who they thought was stirring up the people and leading them astray. The Jewish leaders thought Jesus might enter Jerusalem unnoticed by mingling among the crowds, so they sent spies through Jerusalem to see if they could spot Him.

However Jesus was planning to arrive quite openly. When He and His disciples were a little way off, on the Mount of Olives, Jesus sent two of His friends into the village of Bethphage to find a donkey for him to ride. "You will find one tethered to a doorway," He told them. "Untie it and bring it to me. If anyone objects, just explain that it's me who needs it and they won't stop you."

The disciples found the donkey, just as He had said. When the owners heard who wanted it, they brought it to Jesus themselves. They even threw their cloaks onto its back to make a comfortable saddle for Him to sit on. The little animal had never been ridden before, but it stood calm and willing as Jesus climbed onto it.

Jesus patted the donkey's head, then set off for the city of Jerusalem. When people along the way saw Him coming, they cheered, sang and danced for joy. The ancient prophets had said that the Messiah would ride into Jerusalem on a donkey. And so the people realized that Jesus was claiming openly for the first time that He was the saviour they had been waiting for.

"Hosanna!" they shouted, lining the donkey's path with their cloaks and palm leaves. "Blessed is He who comes in the name of the Lord! Hosanna in the highest!"

People jammed the streets to welcome Jesus all the way into Jerusalem.

"This is outrageous!" the furious Pharisees bellowed at Jesus. "You're making these people think you're the Messiah!"

"Even if they were quiet," Jesus replied, "the stones themselves would cry out to greet me."

Matthew chapter 21; Mark chapter 11; Luke chapter 19; John chapters 11, 12

Jesus and the Temple Traders

As all good Jews did at the feast of Passover, Jesus went to pray at the great temple. He expected to see the courtyards filled with respectful worshippers deep in prayer, moving quietly about so as not to disturb others. Instead, Jesus was horrified to find the sacred building being used as a market-place.

Everywhere He looked, there were stallholders selling doves and other animals for sacrifices. They cried out their wares, competing for business. People bartered with them, trying to get the best prices, while doves cooed and lambs bleated. Among the stalls were money-changers, haggling with worshippers and counting out foreign money into Jewish shekels. All the traders were charging unfair prices, and the worshippers had no choice but to pay. Everyone had to offer a sacrifice and give shekels to the temple funds at Passover. Meanwhile, city traders were using the temple courtyards and corridors to get from one side of Jerusalem to another.

As Jesus stood amid the hubbub, he grew more and more furious. Suddenly, He began sending the traders' tables flying into the air, kicking down stalls, smashing dove cages open and ripping animal tethers loose. "This is the house of God, but you have turned it into a robbers' den!" He yelled, clearing the temple of everyone except for genuine worshippers.

It wasn't long before the courtyards were full again. This time, with people who had come to hear Jesus preach.

Matthew chapter 21; Luke chapter 19

432

Jesus Against the Authorities

Every day of Passover week Jesus stood in the temple preaching to huge crowds and healing many people too. The Jewish leaders were enraged. "Who gives you the right to say and do these things?" they demanded. "Listen to what the people are saying about you – they think you are the Messiah! We are warning you to stop." They sent holy men such as the Pharisees and Sadducees to try to make Jesus break the law in some way so they could arrest Him. But Jesus waged a war of words on them and won every time.

"Holy men such as the Pharisees say that you should follow the rules of Moses," He told everyone one day. "This is right, so listen to what they say. But don't do as they do because they don't practise what they preach!"

People in the crowd began to argue angrily with each other – the Jewish leaders and their followers on one side, and Jesus and His disciples on the other.

Jesus continued, "Everything the holy

men do is for show. They say aloud long prayers in public so everyone can admire them. They wear fancy robes so they stand out in the crowd. They sit at the front at the synagogue and expect to be addressed as 'Teacher'. But I say you have only one teacher – your Father in Heaven, and under Him, everyone is equal. Anyone who thinks they are better than others will one day find themselves the lowest. And anyone who serves others will one day find themselves the greatest."

Jesus criticized the Jewish elders in many other ways, leaving the people in uproar as they debated whether He was right or wrong. "Look at that lady over there," Jesus tried to explain. He pointed to a tiny, bent-over old woman in tatty clothes, shuffling to the temple collection box. With gnarled, trembling fingers, she dropped in a couple of copper coins and prayed. "That old woman is better than all the Jewish leaders," Jesus announced. "They only give what they can afford to charity, leaving plenty for themselves. This woman has hardly anything, but she has still given to God."

The Jewish leaders were determined to somehow seize Jesus. Every day He was surrounded by people in the temple. And every night He stayed outside the city, at Bethany. Jesus was safe for now.

Matthew chapters 21, 23; Mark chapter 12; Luke chapters 19, 21

The Last Supper

The Jewish leaders were extremely frustrated at their failure to get rid of Jesus. One night they gathered at the house of the chief priest, Caiaphas, for an emergency meeting. They were in the middle of discussing what they could do next when there was a knock at the door.

A servant ushered in a most unexpected guest. It was Judas Iscariot, one of Jesus' twelve disciples and closest friends.

"I'm here because I can give you what you want," he said, his eyes glinting coldly. "Jesus of Nazareth – how much is He worth to you?"

The Jewish officials didn't know what had made Judas become a traitor – and they didn't care either. They could hardly believe their good luck. They put their heads together for a few moments and then announced, "Thirty pieces of silver."

Without a word, Judas held out his hand and Caiaphas counted out the coins. From then on, Judas stayed by Jesus' side, waiting for the opportunity to betray Him.

Mysteriously, Jesus knew everything.
With a heavy heart, He prepared for one
last meal with his disciples – the Passover
supper. He organized a room in secret, so
that the Jewish leaders would not find out
where He was, and only told His twelve
friends about it at the last minute.

The disciples were in a very serious
mood as they gathered together. After all,
Jesus had warned them two days earlier
that He was about to fall into the hands of
His enemies and be put to death. As
everything Jesus said came true, they were
extremely worried.

While they settled at the table, Jesus
wrapped a towel around his waist and filled
a bowl with water. The disciples were

shocked to realize He was going to wash the dust from their feet – a job usually done by the very lowliest servant. Peter was especially shocked and tried to stop Jesus kneeling before him, but Jesus insisted. "I am setting you all an example," Jesus said afterwards. "Always put others before yourself."

Then it was time for dinner. Jesus took a loaf of bread and asked for God's blessing over it. "This is my body," He said with great sadness, "which will be given up for you." He broke the bread and gave it to all the disciples to eat. Then Jesus poured a cup of wine and asked for God's blessing over that too. "This is my blood," He announced gravely, "the sign of a new promise from

God. My blood will be spilt so that everyone's sins will be forgiven." One by one, the disciples took the cup and drank.

Then Jesus gestured for everyone to begin sharing out the different dishes on the

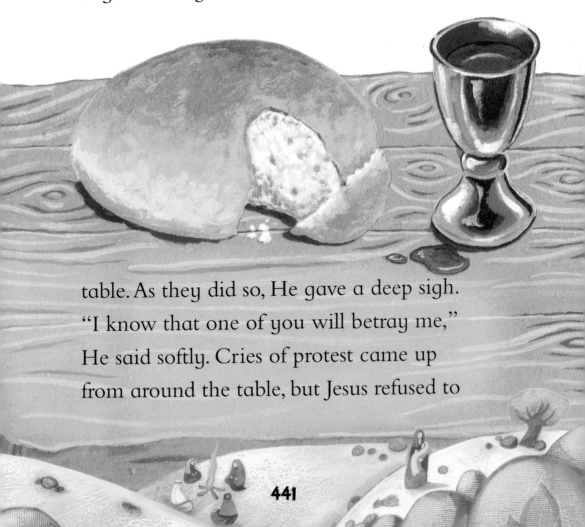

table. As they did so, He gave a deep sigh. "I know that one of you will betray me," He said softly. Cries of protest came up from around the table, but Jesus refused to explain further. As the disciples reluctantly turned back to eating, Peter murmured to John, who was sitting closest to Jesus, "Ask Him which of us He means."

John leaned over and spoke in Jesus' ear.

He whispered back, "The one to whom I will give this piece of bread."

John told Peter, and they watched as Jesus tore some bread and offered it to Judas Iscariot. "Do whatever you have to," Jesus told His disloyal friend, "but do it quickly."

And without a word Judas got up from the table and left the room.

Matthew chapter 26; Mark chapter 14; Luke chapter 22; John chapter 13

The Garden of Gethsemane

After Jesus had shared His last supper with the disciples, He sat back and looked around at His dear friends. "I give you a new commandment," He said. "Love each other as I have loved you. By doing this, everyone will know that you are my followers."

"Lord, you've been talking all night as if you're leaving us," Peter protested.

"Yes," Jesus said gently. "I am going away, and where I am going you won't be able to follow me – for a while, at least."

"Why can't I follow you now?" Peter cried out. "I am ready to die for you!"

But Jesus smiled sadly. "Are you really, my friend?" He asked. "By the time this night is out and the cock has crowed three times at dawn, you will have denied three times that you even know me."

"Never," Peter said, choking with sorrow. "Never." And all the disciples agreed strongly.

"Don't be upset," Jesus tried to comfort them. "I am going to prepare a place for you in my Father's house. And I will return to you for a short while, before I have to go away again for good. Even then when you will no longer be able to see me, I will always live in your hearts. Later, when the time is right, you will follow and we will be together again. Until then, do what I have done tonight as a way of remembering me. Be at peace, and be happy for me that I am going to be with my Father."

Jesus looked around at His friends' gloomy faces.

"Now come," He said gently. "Let's go to the Mount of Olives. I would like to pray in the Garden of Gethsemane for a while."

As they walked through the moonlight together, Jesus gave the disciples many more important instructions. He knew He only had a short time left in which to talk to them. When they finally reached the entrance to the Garden of Gethsemane, Jesus saw that the anxious men were exhausted. "Rest here while I go and pray," He told most of them. But He turned to Peter, James and John and said, "I know you are tired, but would you come with me?"

The three were only too pleased to keep Jesus company. They had never seen Him look so strained and troubled before.

"My heart feels like it's breaking," Jesus sighed heavily when they had gone a little way. "Will you stay while I pray?"

Peter, James and John watched as Jesus sank to his knees, His head in His hands.

"Father!" He cried silently. Jesus prayed
that perhaps He might not
have to face the suffering
He knew lay ahead.

After a long while, Jesus
turned to Peter, James and John
but saw they had fallen asleep.

So Jesus prayed again. He
felt the sins of all the world
weighing on His shoulders and He knew
the full horror of what was to come.

Once more Jesus turned to his friends,
but they were still asleep.

And Jesus prayed again, willingly
accepting the suffering He had to face, so
that all people could one day reach God.

At last Jesus finished praying. Peter, James

and John were still asleep. But at that
moment Judas Iscariot arrived,
accompanied by a band of guards. At the
noise of guards' swords and chains and the
light from their flaming torches, the disciples
woke up, startled. "Master," Judas said
calmly, greeting Jesus with his usual kiss.

At that pre-arranged sign, the guards
grabbed Jesus. After a brief commotion and
panic, the disciples fled for their lives into
the darkness.

Matthew chapter 26; Mark chapter 14; Luke chapter 22; John chapters 13, 14, 18

Peter Denies Jesus

Surrounded by soldiers with weapons at the ready, that night Jesus was marched into the city of Jerusalem. Behind them, stumbling through the shadows went Peter, not letting his friend out of his sight for a second. He even followed when they reached the great house of the high priest,

Caiaphas. The guards marched Jesus into the front courtyard. But then the big doors opened, Jesus was hauled inside, and they banged shut. Peter could go no further.

How helpless Peter felt now! He had a sword with him in the Garden of Gethsemane, and slashing wildly he had managed to injure one of the guards, cutting off his ear. But Jesus shouted at him to stop, saying that violence was wrong. Jesus touched the soldier's ear and it had been instantly healed. Now Peter could do nothing except wait to see what happened.

Keeping his head down, Peter edged into a small group of servants and maids stood around a bonfire nearby. He sat quietly, trying not to draw attention to himself, wondering what terrors Jesus was facing.

"I know you," came a voice. Peter ignored it but the voice spoke again. "You're friends with the prisoner, Jesus of Galilee." It was a serving girl and she was pointing right at him.

"No I wasn't," Peter said, his heart suddenly racing. "You must have me confused with someone else."

"Yes, you were. I've seen you with him too," said another maid. And everyone stared at Peter and began mumbling to each other.

"I don't know him, I tell you," Peter said, his voice rising louder than he intended.

"You must be a follower of Jesus of Nazareth," accused a man right beside him.

"After all, you speak with the same accent as Him."

"I said I don't know anyone of that name!" Peter yelled, and he strode away.

As he did so dawn began to break and the sound of a cockerel crowing ripped through the air – once… twice… three times. Peter's head span as he remembered Jesus' words. "By the time this night is out and the cock has crowed three times at dawn, you will have denied three times that you even know me." Sobbing with shame, loss and fear, Peter ran away.

Matthew chapter 26; Mark chapter 14;
Luke chapter 22; John chapter 18

Jesus on Trial

Inside Caiaphas' mansion, Jesus was quizzed by Annas, the former high priest. What did He think about ancient holy writings? What miracles did He claim to have worked? Who did He think He was?

Jesus refused to answer and was marched to a room full of Jewish officials. They had witnesses who they had paid to lie, accusing Jesus of saying and doing things that were against Jewish law. But the witnesses couldn't get their stories straight!

Finally Caiaphas hissed, "I order you to tell us, under solemn oath, whether you think you are the Son of God."

"I am," He said with grace, "and one day you will see the Son of Man seated at the right hand of the Father in Heaven."

"Blasphemy!" roared Caiaphas, a satisfied gleam in his eyes. Blasphemy was the crime of lying against God for which the punishment was death.

In triumph, the Jewish elders had Jesus blindfolded. They slapped and kicked Him, shouting, "Prophesy for us now, Messiah.

Guess who hit you!" And in the morning, they had Jesus brought in front of the Roman governor, Pontius Pilate. Only he could approve an execution.

The news spread around the city and an enormous crowd gathered outside.

Pilate asked Jesus many more questions. Are you really a king? Have you been plotting against the Roman government? Have you been planning a rebellion?

Perplexed, Pilate couldn't find that Jesus had done anything wrong. He ordered that Jesus also be questioned by Herod, the ruler of Galilee, who was in Jerusalem at that time. But Herod couldn't find Jesus guilty of anything either. Even Pilate's wife told him that she had had a dream in which Jesus of

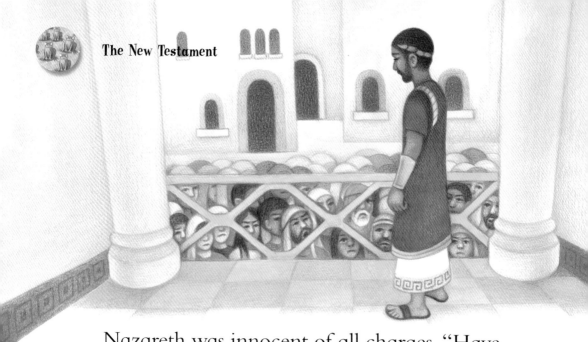

Nazareth was innocent of all charges. "Have nothing further to do with him," she advised her husband.

Pilate made his decision. He went out onto the balcony of his judgement hall and announced to the waiting crowds, "This man has done nothing to deserve death. He shall be whipped and let go." And Jesus was dragged off for His punishment.

Meanwhile the Jewish officials had mingled with the crowds, persuading them that Jesus was guilty of blasphemy. As Pilate turned to go back into his Judgement Hall, people sent up cries of, "Kill him! Kill Jesus of Nazareth!"

But the Roman governor was deeply disturbed, he did not know what for.

Suddenly he had an idea. Pilate remembered that it was Passover and there was a custom for the governor to release one prisoner of the people's choice. In the cells was a murderer called Barabbas. Pilate felt sure that the people would rather have Jesus released than a violent killer.

"Who shall I pardon – Barabbas or Jesus of Nazareth?" Pilate asked the crowd.

He couldn't believe his ears when the shouts came back, "Barabbas!"

Pilate ordered that Jesus be brought in front of him once more. He had been whipped until blood poured down His back. The guards had mocked him as the King of the Jews, too, by pressing a crown of thorns onto His head and throwing a cloak around his shoulders.

Now the crowd jeered too.

Pilate had had enough. He called for water and a towel, and washed his hands in front of everyone. "I cleanse myself of this man's blood," he announced.

Then Barabbas was released and Jesus was led away to be crucified.

Matthew chapters 26, 27; Mark chapters 14, 15;
Luke chapters 22, 23; John chapters 18, 19

The Crucifixion

Jesus had withstood being marched about in chains, hours of angry questioning, a beating from the Jewish officials, and being brutally whipped by Pilate's guards. The crown of thorns was still pressed into His head, sending blood trickling down His pained-filled face.

Two Roman soldiers lifted a huge, solid wooden cross over Jesus' shoulder — so heavy that He nearly collapsed from the weight of it. Then Jesus staggered onwards, through the streets of Jerusalem and towards the hill outside the city where He and two other criminals were to be executed.

Thousands of people lined the way, watching the procession. Jesus willed Himself forwards, heavy step after heavy step. But eventually He crashed into the dust, utterly exhausted. The angry guards dragged a strong man from the crowd called Simon of Cyrene and ordered him to carry the cross instead.

People in the crowd yelled insults and spat on Jesus as He stumbled by. But Jesus caught sight of the sorrowful faces of many friends He had made too. Many of the women were weeping. "Don't cry for me," Jesus said, "but for yourselves, your children and for the destruction that is to come."

Eventually they reached the place for the execution. It was called Golgotha, meaning 'place of the skull'. A soldier made Jesus lie down on the cross, and long nails were hammered into His hands and feet. "Father forgive them, for they don't know what they are doing," Jesus moaned. A notice was fixed above his head which said 'Jesus of Nazareth, King of the Jews' in three languages. "It shouldn't say that," some

Jewish officials objected. "It should say 'This man said he was the King of the Jews'."

But the Roman governor, Pilate, boomed, "I ordered it to be written just like that and that is the way it will stay!"

The Jewish officials mocked as Jesus' cross was hoisted up high. "You said you're the Son of God – so save yourself!"

As the two criminals were raised on crosses either side of Jesus, one sneered, "Yes, save yourself and save us too!"

"How dare you!" the second thief groaned. "We deserve this, but Jesus is innocent. Lord, remember me when you reach your kingdom."

"I promise you," whispered Jesus, "today you will be with me in paradise."

Even though it was midday, darkness suddenly fell over the land. Close by at the foot of the cross, was Jesus' heartbroken mother, and His close friends including John, Mary Magdalene and Salome.

"Mother, take care of John as if he were your own son," Jesus murmered. "John, look after my mother as if she were your own."

Jesus hung in agony on the cross for three long hours. Then He lifted His head and cried aloud, "My God! Why have you abandoned me?" Somebody rushed to lift a stick with a sponge on the end that had been dipped in wine so He could have a drink. Jesus cried out again, "Father, I give up my spirit into your hands. It is finished." And His head drooped.

At that very moment, the earth rumbled and shook, and rocks split open. People said that the great curtain in the temple ripped from top to bottom. Others said they saw graves open and spirits rise from them.

A Roman officer at the foot of the cross looked up and gasped, "This man truly was the Son of God."

Matthew chapter 27; Mark chapter 15; Luke chapter 23; John chapter 19

The First Easter

The evening after Jesus had been put to death, a wealthy Jew called Joseph of Arimathea begged Pontius Pilate to allow him to bury Jesus' body. Pilate agreed. So Joseph went with his friend, Nicodemus, back to Golgotha, where women were still weeping at the foot of His cross. Gently,

Joseph and Nicodemus lifted Jesus' poor, bleeding body down. They wrapped Him in a linen shroud with burial spices and, accompanied by the sobbing women, took Him to a nearby cemetery. There the two men laid Jesus in a small, cave-like tomb that Joseph had already paid for, and rolled a heavy stone across the entrance. Full of grief and with nothing else to do, they left.

Meanwhile, some Jewish officials had been to see Pilate. "Jesus of Nazareth said He would rise up again after three days," they told the Roman governor. "Have soldiers guard His tomb so no one can steal the body, then tell everyone that He's miraculously come back to life." Pilate nodded and sent the men away.

Pilate's guards sat outside Jesus' tomb through the night of that first Good Friday – nothing happened. They kept watch all the next day and again nobody came. But as dawn broke on the Sabbath, the third day, the earth suddenly shook so violently that it knocked the soldiers off their feet. A white light blazed out of the sky and shone over the tomb. Through the glare, the terrified soldiers watched the glowing figure of a man roll away the massive stone from the tomb entrance. The soldiers were scared by what they saw and fled for their lives.

Not long afterwards a group of grieving women arrived at the cemetery to pay their respects at the tomb. They included Jesus' friends Mary Magdalene, Mary the mother

of James and John, Salome and Joanna.
When they saw that the soldiers were gone
and the stone had been rolled away, they
screamed in horror.

Someone must have
stolen Jesus' body!
Inside the tomb
where Jesus' body
should have been, two
shining men were
sitting. "Why are you
looking for the living
among the dead?" the
men said. "Don't you
remember that the Son of Man said He
would rise on the third day?"

Mary Magdalene raced to fetch the

disciples Peter and John. When the two men saw the empty tomb they were full of anger. They went off to try to find out who had taken the body. Mary sank down outside the tomb, sobbing. Then suddenly she sensed someone behind her. Mary span around and, through her tears she saw a blurry figure whom she thought must be the cemetery gardener. "Why are you weeping?" the man asked.

"If you moved the body," she begged, "please tell me where to."

The man said just one word.

"Mary."

Mary's heart stood still. Suddenly, she recognized the man – it was Jesus!

"Go now," Jesus said softly, as Mary fell

at His feet, gazing up at Him in wonder. "Find the disciples and tell them that I will soon be returning to my Father."

Meanwhile, the other women who had seen the empty tomb were hurrying homewards when all at once, a man appeared out of nowhere on the road in front of them. "Good morning," He said.

The women were amazed and couldn't believe who they were hearing and seeing.

"Don't be afraid," Jesus said. "Go and tell my disciples to travel to Galilee and I will meet them there soon."

Matthew chapters 27, 28; Mark chapter 16; Luke chapters 23, 24; John chapters 19, 20

Jesus and Doubting Thomas

Late morning on the third day after Jesus' death, Mary Magdalene burst into the room where the grieving disciples sat together. "I have seen Jesus!" she cried, flushed with excitement, and told them everything that had happened at the tomb. But as much as the disciples wanted to believe her, they couldn't.

Meanwhile, two of Jesus' disciples were on their way from Jerusalem to the nearby village of Emmaus. As they walked with heavy hearts, a stranger joined them and began talking. To the disciples' astonishment, the stranger didn't seem to have heard anything of the events everyone was talking about – the death of Jesus and the disappearance of His body. However, he seemed to know the ancient holy writings very well and began explaining them.

"Don't you know that the holy men of old said that the Messiah would have to suffer to win glory?"

Later on the disciples shared a meal with the stranger and he blessed some bread,

broke it into pieces and gave it to them.
It was only then that they realized who he
really was. "Jesus!" they gasped in
astonishment. And at that moment, He
disappeared.

The disciples hurried back to the city
and went straight to tell the others – only to
find that Jesus had appeared to Peter too!

Everyone began talking at once, full of
excitement and asking to hear the stories
again and again. No one noticed the
newcomer arrive in their midst.

"Peace be with you," said Jesus, as
everyone stood back in fear as though He
was a ghost. "Don't be frightened," He
said, "it's me. Look – here are the wounds
on my hands and feet."

But one disciple was missing – Thomas. When his friends told him what had happened he didn't believe it. Eight days later everyone was gathered again to talk and pray. Halfway through the meeting, Jesus appeared once more. "See for yourself, Thomas," He said. "Come and touch my wounds. Have faith – it's true."

Thomas broke down. "My Lord, it's really you," he sobbed.

"Bless you for believing," Jesus said gently. "But even more blessed are those who won't see me and yet will still believe."

Matthew chapter 28; Mark chapter 16;
Luke chapter 24; John chapter 20

The Stranger on the Beach

One evening, some of the disciples gathered at the Sea of Galilee. Peter wanted to take a little boat out and go fishing, just as he used to do in the days when he was a fisherman. Soon he and his friends, including James, John, Thomas and Nathaniel, were sailing out into open waters under a starry sky. How free and peaceful it felt – a welcome relief from the terrible events in the city in recent weeks.

All night, the disciples waited for fish to fill their nets, but when dawn came, they were all empty.

Then a voice floated across the waves. "Have you caught anything?"

Peering into the distance, the disciples could see the figure of a man on the shore.

"No, nothing." they yelled back.

"Try dropping your nets to the right side of the boat," came the voice.

The disciples thought it was worth a try. They soon felt their nets become heavy and they could hardly lift them.

Peter, James and John looked at each

other and they remembered a time in the past when exactly the same thing had happened. "It's Jesus!" they exclaimed. Peter couldn't wait to finish hauling in the catch and sail to shore, so he dived straight into the water and swam to be the first to reach Jesus. Before long, Peter and the rest of the friends joined Jesus on the shore, and gathered around a little fire on the beach. They sat roasting fish for breakfast, and it was just like old times.

John chapter 21

The Ascension into Heaven

It was finally time for Jesus to leave the world for good. He gathered his disciples together and walked to the Mount of Olives, a short way from Jerusalem.

"Stay in the city for a while," Jesus told His eleven old friends. "You have already all been baptized once – by John the Baptist, with water. But soon you will all be baptized again – this time with the Holy Spirit. God is going to send you powerful gifts and I want you to use them by going out into the world and telling people in every country about me. Baptize all those who believe in me as my followers, in the name of the Father, the Son and the Holy Spirit. Teach them everything that I have taught you." Jesus looked at His friends' worried faces. "Don't forget," He said gently, "I will be with you always, until the end of time."

With that, Jesus rose up into the air, higher and higher, until He disappeared into a blazing cloud of glory.

As the disciples squinted up at the

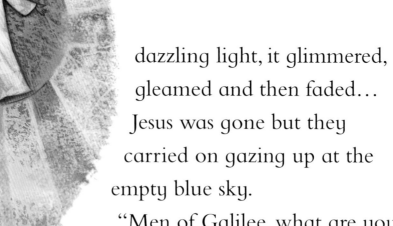

dazzling light, it glimmered, gleamed and then faded…

Jesus was gone but they carried on gazing up at the empty blue sky.

"Men of Galilee, what are you looking at?" came a voice. The disciples turned to find two men in glowing robes standing next to them.

"Jesus has gone, but one day He will come back to you in the same way."

Full of wonder and sadness, the disciples were comforted and made their way back to Jerusalem. They knew they would not see Jesus again soon, but were sure that one day He would return in glory.

Matthew chapter 28; Mark chapter 16; Luke chapter 24; Acts chapter 1

The Coming of the Holy Spirit

The disciples were in Jerusalem waiting for the Holy Spirit to come and baptize them, as Jesus had told them. Meanwhile they decided to replace the traitor, Judas Iscariot, with a new disciple. Then they would be twelve once more, as Jesus had originally intended. They prayed for guidance, and cast votes and Matthias was chosen. The twelve became known as the apostles. Then the waiting continued.

Fifty days after Passover and the death of Jesus, it was the feast of Pentecost – when Jews celebrated how God had given their religious laws to Moses. The apostles were celebrating the feast, when suddenly a mighty sound like a rushing wind filled their ears as though it was all around them in the house. The apostles felt alive and full of energy, and turning to each other in astonishment, they saw that every man had a tiny flame hovering over his head.

"It must be the Holy Spirit!" they cried,

and they found they were
all speaking in different
languages.

Realizing they had been
blessed with the special gifts Jesus
has talked about, the apostles
excitedly ran out into the streets.
Some found themselves giving thanks
to God in Greek. Others were
preaching about Jesus in Latin. Some
were praising the Holy Spirit in Arabic, and
many other languages.

Many worshippers from foreign lands
had come to Jerusalem for Pentecost and
they were stunned. "These men are from
Galilee!" they marvelled. "How can they
speak our language?"

However, some people just laughed and said that the apostles were drunk.

Then Peter began preaching and everyone who heard him was stirred by his passion. "We are not drunk," he laughed. "We are followers of Jesus of Nazareth. He has risen from the dead, we have seen it with our own eyes. Today we have been blessed by the Holy Spirit with these gifts of languages. Anyone who is truly sorry for their sins and follows the teachings of Jesus will be blessed too. Who wants to join us?"

That day the apostles baptized over three thousand people as followers of Jesus. The foundations of the Christian Church had been laid.

Acts chapters 1, 2

Miracles and
Persecution

Every day after Pentecost, the apostles preached and worked miracles. And each day, more people were baptized as followers of Jesus.

One day, Peter and John were on their way into the temple to pray when they were stopped by a crippled beggar, asking for a few coins. "We have no money," Peter explained, "but what we do have I will give you… In the name of Jesus, get up and walk!" Peter reached out for the beggar's hand and encouraged him to get to his feet. The ragged man stood up and took a few unsteady paces. Then he began to dance with joy – and he danced all the way into the temple behind Peter and John.

The many worshippers there were utterly amazed. So Peter began speaking aloud, telling everyone about Jesus, how He had risen from the dead and about their God-given gifts of healing. Suddenly, some Jewish officials appeared. They were furious that the name of Jesus was once more causing a commotion among everyone in

the temple. They had Peter and John thrown
into prison for two days. But the men had
committed no crime so they were freed.

Like all of the apostles, Peter did many
astounding things in Jesus' name. He seemed
to know things that he couldn't possibly
know – unless God Himself had told him.
He also performed many other
great miracles of healing.

Sick people came from
all over the country to sit
in the streets of Jerusalem
just in case Peter passed
by. They believed that
even if his shadow fell
upon them, they would be cured. Of course,
this enraged the Jewish officials further. Jesus

was dead, but His name was still stirring up the people so the Jewish officials put Peter and John in prison once more. However that very night they found that the two men had vanished! Upon finding the two apostles teaching in the temple, the Jewish officials' explanation was that an angel had come and released them. The confused, furious officials then had Peter and John beaten, and ordered them never to speak the name of Jesus again.

Of course, this didn't stop the apostles. Every day, the number of followers of Jesus grew. The time came when the Jewish officials finally decided that enough was enough and they accused one apostle, Stephen, of blasphemy and stoned him to death. He was the first man ever to die in the name of Jesus. Next they sent soldiers to every house in Jerusalem, and then through the rest of Judea too, searching for other followers to arrest. Little did the officials know they were part of God's great plan. The apostles fled to safety to lands far and wide, taking the word of Jesus to many thousands of people who wouldn't otherwise have heard it.

Acts chapters 2, 4, 5, 7, 8

A Narrow Escape

As he travelled around, Peter worked many miracles in the name of Jesus. In a town called Lydda, in north-east Judea, he healed a paralyzed man. In the town of Joppa, he brought Tabitha, a woman who had died, back to life. Only Jesus Himself and the great prophets Elijah

and Elisha had ever been granted this gift.
Peter preached to Jews and non Jews alike,
because he knew that everyone was equal
in the eyes of God. He also baptized the
first non Jews to follow Jesus.

Meanwhile, King Herod Agrippa
became just as determined as the Jewish
officials to get rid of the 'trouble-making'
Christians. He was a wicked man and he
had James, the brother of John, put to
death. Then he had Peter the leader of the
apostles arrested and put on trial. Flung
into a dungeon, Peter was chained to two
soldiers, with a round-the-clock guard
outside his door. Herod heard how Peter
and John had escaped from prison before,
and was taking no chances.

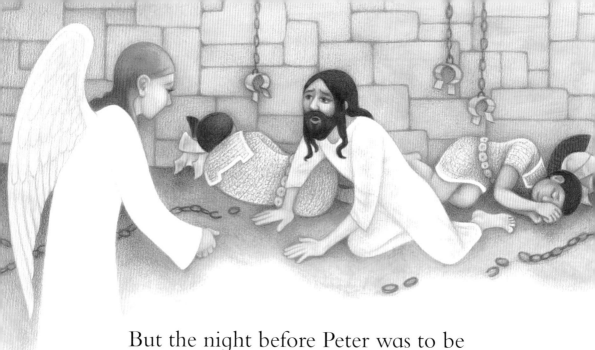

But the night before Peter was to be tried, he dreamt that a light blazed into his cell and an angel woke him. "Get up quickly!" the angel commanded. Peter felt his chains fall away, realizing that it wasn't a dream. Then he followed the angel past the guards and out into the street.

The next day, when Herod heard of Peter's escape, he sent soldiers out after him. But Peter was nowhere to be found.

Acts chapters 9, 10, 12

The Road
to Damascus

One of the Jewish officers who was determined to wipe out Christians was a young man called Saul. He became famous and feared as a ruthless persecutor of the followers of Jesus. Saul had been brought up as a Pharisee – a very strict Jew – and he felt that Jesus' apostles were

undoing all the ancient laws he held to be
important. Saul had decided to seek out
Christians – not just in Jerusalem, or even
Judea, but in other countries too. He went
to the high priest in Jerusalem and asked for
letters of introduction to the synagogues in
Damascus, the capital of Syria, so he could
find and arrest followers of Jesus there.

Soon Saul was on his way. As the great
city loomed before him, a flash of lightning
blazed from the sky and struck him off his
horse. Saul grovelled in the dirt, shaken to
the core. Somehow he knew it hadn't been
an accident.

"Saul, Saul, why are you persecuting
me?" a voice boomed into his mind.

"Who – who are you?" the terrified Saul

managed to stutter, shutting his eyes against the dazzle.

"I am Jesus, whom you have sworn to persecute," the voice roared. "Now get up, go into the city and wait there."

The voice was gone, the light faded and Saul opened his eyes.

Everything was black… He was blind!

The soldiers accompanying Saul were puzzled. They led him into the city and found a place for him to stay. There Saul sat for two days, refusing to talk to anyone or even eat or drink.

On the third day, there was a knock at the door. Saul's soldiers opened it to an old man named Ananias. "God has sent me to you," Ananias explained. "He told me that He has chosen you to spread His message – not just to the Jews, but to non Jews too."

Gently, Ananias laid his hands on Saul's head and the darkness gradually became light, as if scales fell from his eyes, and he could see again.

Overwhelmed with relief and joy, Saul fell to his knees and gave thanks to God. Then he asked Ananias to baptize him!

When Saul had recovered from his ordeal, he went straight to the synagogues of Damascus, as he had planned. But instead of arresting Christians, he preached that Jesus was the Son of God.

Acts chapters 8, 9

Paul and Silas in Prison

At first, people found it difficult to believe that Saul had gone from being a sworn enemy of Jesus to one of his most passionate followers. To give people an outward sign of his change of heart, Saul changed his name to Paul. He managed to win trust by putting even more energy and effort into finding new followers for Jesus. As a Pharisee, Paul had great knowledge of the ancient sacred writings, and could argue in support of Jesus with the Jewish officials in Jerusalem too. How they came to hate their former favourite, Saul! Eventually the apostles discovered that the officials were plotting to kill Paul, so they sent him far to the north to the city of Tarsus, where he could preach out of danger.

That was the beginning of many years of travelling for Paul, teaching the messages of Jesus to people all around the Mediterranean. Often accompanied by other apostles, such as Barnabas and John, he made one journey after another. He taught non Jews about God, from Syria to

Cyprus, and Turkey to Greece, and baptized
thousands in the name of Jesus. However
Paul and his friends faced many dangers.
Angry Jews hated them for baptizing non
Jews, and non Jews hated them for saying
that the idols they worshipped were false.
Even when Paul and his companions were
chased out of town, or suffered violence,
they weren't put off. In fact they became
even more determined. Every single soul
they won for God gave them great joy.

Paul and his fellow apostle Silas were
once in Macedonia when they were
accused of 'disturbing the peace', and were
whipped and thrown into prison. However
they refused to be downhearted. They
began singing hymns to God, and the other

prisoners joined in too.

At midnight, the sudden sound of
rumbling drowned out the apostles' voices.

The prison walls shook and started to
crumble. The terrified prisoners were thrown
from side to side. Their chains broke and
their cell doors burst open.

All the prisoners could have seized the opportunity to escape, but Paul and Silas talked everyone into staying put. When the jailer ran in with his guards, he couldn't believe it. He had been ready to take his own life if all of the prisoners had run away while under his responsibility. The jailer ordered for them to be chained up again, all except for Paul and Silas who were taken to his house. There, the jailer fell on his knees before them and asked them to tell him more about Jesus.

By the time dawn came, the jailer and his whole household had been baptized.

Acts chapters 10, 11, 13 to 16

Paul at Sea

Paul became well known for having mysterious powers and working great miracles of healing. He once brought a boy called Eutychus back to life, who had died by falling out of a window.

Before returning to Jerusalem one year for the feast of Pentecost, the Holy Spirit warned him that imprisonment and suffering lay ahead. Paul was not scared. He was ready to die for Jesus if he needed to.

In Jerusalem the Jewish officials had Paul arrested for supposedly breaking holy rules. They accused him of encouraging Jewish Christians to ignore the ancient laws of Moses. They also accused him of sneaking non Jews into the sacred temple – all untrue charges. Paul found himself in prison yet again, with enemies who wanted him dead. Eventually, he was freed, but he was placed under house arrest and unable to go anywhere for two years. Finally Paul had enough. He had been born in Rome and as a Roman citizen he claimed his right to be tried by the emperor himself.

Paul set sail for Rome, but on the voyage his ship ran into a raging storm. In a dream an angel told him the ship would sink but everyone would survive. And so it happened. The ship was tossed onto a sandbank and battered by waves. All of the people onboard were washed up alive on the island of Malta. On finally reaching Rome, Paul was put under house arrest again, for a further two years. So he spent his time writing letters to friends, urging them to live good lives and trust in God. And that's how Paul lived until he was finally put to death.

Acts chapters 17 to 28

John's Vision of Heaven

The apostle John was praying one day, when he heard a voice say, "Write down what I am going to show you and send it to the followers of Jesus."

John span around, and there was Jesus, shining with light. Jesus said, "Don't be afraid. I am the first and the last. I am the

505

Living One who was dead. Now I shall live forever. Watch – I will show you the future."

John saw a door opening into Heaven, revealing God surrounded by singing angels.

He was shown marvel after marvel. The battle between good and evil playing out on the Earth, and the end of the world when Jesus was triumphant, hurling the devil into a lake of fire. John saw God passing judgement on all who had ever lived. If a person's name was not in the Lord's great book, they were destroyed with their master, Satan.

Then John was shown a new Heaven
and Earth, and out of Heaven came a
vision of a new Jerusalem. The city gleamed
and glittered as though it was made from
gold and jewels. Through the city flowed the
River of Life, its water as clear as crystal.
God Himself was living there. His Kingdom
on Earth had come.

John heard Jesus speaking one last time.
"I will be coming soon, and I shall
reward the good with blessings forever."

And John whispered, "Amen!"

Revelation chapters 1, 4, 5, 19 to 22

People in the Bible

Aaron The brother of Moses. He helped Moses to lead the Israelites out of captivity in Egypt.

Abel Adam and Eve's second son, a shepherd. He was murdered by his brother Cain, out of jealousy.

Abram (Abraham) A descendant of Noah. God changed his name to Abraham and promised that he would be the father of God's Chosen People.

Adam The first man on Earth, created by God.

Andrew Fisherman and brother of Peter, who became one of Jesus' twelve apostles.

Bartholomew One of Jesus' twelve apostles.

Cain Adam and Eve's first son, a crop farmer. He killed his brother Abel in a jealous rage.

Daniel Among the Israelites taken captive into Babylon. God gave him the power to interpret dreams and he became chief advisor to several kings. Daniel was thrown to the lions but his faith in God saved him from death.

David The youngest son of Jesse, and a shepherd boy. He defeated the giant Philistine warrior Goliath of Gath and became the greatest king of Israel.

Delilah Lover to the Israelite, Samson. Delilah tricked him into giving her the secret of his strength, then handed Samson over to his enemies – the Philistines.

Elijah A great Israelite prophet whom God gave the power to bring a child back from the dead. He was taken up into Heaven in a chariot of flames.

Elisha The follower and companion of Elijah, a great prophet and miracle-worker.

Elizabeth Mother of John the Baptist and cousin of Mary, Jesus' mother.

Esau Isaac and Rebecca's son, and twin brother of Jacob. He was tricked into selling his birthright to Jacob in exchange for a bowl of stew.

Esther An Israelite taken nto captivity in Babylon, who became queen to King Xerxes. She saved the Israelites from execution.

Eve The first woman on Earth, created by God.

Gabriel An angel sent by God to bring messages to people on Earth. He told Mary that she was going to have a baby, and to call Him Jesus.

Gideon An Israelite man whom God showed how to crush an enemy people called the Midianites.

Hagar Maid to Sarah, Abraham's wife, and mother of his first son, Ishmael.

Herod the Great King of Judea at the time Jesus was born. He tried to have Jesus killed.

Isaac Son of Abraham and Sarah, husband of Rebecca and father of twins Esau and Jacob. His father nearly sacrificed Isaac at God's command.

Ishmael Abraham's firstborn and son of Hagar, he became the founder of the Arab nations.

Jacob The younger of Isaac's and Rebecca's twin boys and brother of Esau, whom he tricked out of his birthright. He had twelve sons.

James Brother of John and son of Zebedee, he became one of Jesus' twelve apostles.

James One of Jesus' twelve apostles.

Jeremiah A prophet who foretold that Israel would be conquered by the Babylonians and the people taken into exile as slaves.

John Brother of James and son of Zebedee, who became one of Jesus' twelve apostles. He was granted a vision of the Kingdom of Heaven.

John the Baptist A prophet who preached about the coming of the Messiah and baptized Jesus in the River Jordan.

Jonah An Israelite who was swallowed up by a giant fish as part of a punishment for disobeying God's orders.

Joseph Husband of Mary and foster father of Jesus, he was a carpenter who lived in Nazareth.

Joseph Best-loved son of Jacob. He was sold into slavery by his brothers, but became the King of Egypt's chief minister and was reunited with his family.

Joseph of Arimathea A wealthy Jew and follower of Jesus, who took Jesus' body down from the cross and laid Him in a tomb.

Joshua The leader of the Israelites after Moses, a great army commander who conquered most of Canaan – the Promised Land – for the twelve tribes.

Judas Iscariot One of Jesus' twelve apostles. He betrayed Jesus to His enemies.

Lazarus Brother of Martha and Mary, and friend of Jesus. Jesus raised him from the dead.

Lot Nephew of Abraham who brought Lot up as his own son. God destroyed Lot's town of Sodom and his wife was turned into a pillar of salt.

Martha Sister of Mary and Lazarus, and friend of Jesus. She was a keen follower of Jesus.

Mary Sister of Martha and Lazarus, and friend of Jesus. He and His twelve disciples stayed at their house.

Mary Mother of Jesus and wife of Joseph of Nazareth.

Mary Magdalene A woman who became a good friend of Jesus. She was the first person to see Him after He had risen from the dead.

Matthew Also known as Levi, he was a tax collector who became one of Jesus' twelve apostles.

Moses An Israelite who grew up as an Egyptian prince. With his brother, Aaron, he led the Israelites out of captivity in Egypt, to God's Promised Land of Canaan. He was given the Ten Commandments by God.

Naomi An Israelite widow and mother-in-law to Ruth. God rewarded her for her courage, faith and good behaviour.

Nebuchadnezzar The King of the Babylonians. He conquered the Jewish kingdom of Judah after the Assyrians conquered the Jewish kingdom of Israel.

Noah The man ordered by God to build an ark and load it with creatures and his family – the only living things to be saved when God destroyed the world in a huge flood.

Paul A Pharisee originally called Saul, he was a persecutor of Christians until God worked a miracle that changed his mind. He then changed his name to Paul and devoted his life to spreading the teachings of Jesus to people in many countries around the Mediterranean.

Peter Originally named Simon Peter. He was a fisherman and brother of Andrew, and became one of Jesus' twelve apostles.

Philip Formerly a follower of John the Baptist, he became one of Jesus' twelve apostles.

Pontius Pilate The Roman governor who did not agree with the Jewish officials' death sentence for Jesus, even though he approved it.

Rebecca Isaac's wife and mother of twins Esau and Jacob. She helped Jacob trick his brother out of his birthright.

Ruth A Moabite girl who stayed with her old, poor mother-in-law, Naomi, to look after her when they were both widowed. God later rewarded her for her loyalty.

 Samson An Israelite to whom God gave incredible strength – as long as he did not cut his hair. He was the sworn enemy of the Philistines.

Samuel Brought up as a child by the high priest Eli in the temple, he was chosen by God to be a great prophet.

Sarai (Sarah) Abraham's wife, mother of Isaac. God changed her name to Sarah.

Saul The first king of Israel, who was punished by God.

Simeon An old holy man who had been promised by God that he would not die until he had seen the Messiah, Jesus.

Simon the Zealot One of Jesus' twelve apostles.

Solomon The son of King David, who became the third King of Israel. God gave him the gift of wisdom. He built the first great temple in Jerusalem.

Stephen The first ever person to be put to death for being a follower of Jesus. He was later made a saint.

Thaddeus One of Jesus' twelve apostles.

Thomas One of Jesus' twelve apostles. He didn't believe reports that Jesus had risen from the dead until he had seen Jesus for himself.

Zachariah A priest, and father of John the Baptist.